FALLING BACK TO EARTH

A FIRST HAND ACCOUNT
OF THE GREAT SPACE RACE
AND THE END OF THE COLD WAR

MARK ALBRECHT

ISBN: 0615447090
ISBN-13: 9780615447094

ACKNOWLEDGEMENTS

There are many people who made this book possible and without whose help <u>Falling Back to Earth</u> could never have been written. Starting with Pete Wilson, former U.S. Senator, then Governor of California, always close friend and mentor, who took a risk and gave me the opportunity to be part his Senate team. He is a paragon of public service, good judgment, steel conviction, selfless leadership and an unrivaled team builder. As the journey chronicled in this book unfolded I had reason to pause frequently from what I was doing or about to do and to wonder, "What would Pete do?" Californians are lucky to have had his service over many years...they would do well to repeal the "term limit" and return him to Sacramento.

Dan Quayle, U.S. Senator from Indiana and the 44th Vice President of the United States has had an incalculable influence on my life and this book. Like Pete Wilson, he is a public servant worthy of America's admiration and gratitude; I am honored to call him a friend. Some readers may be surprised at the portrait of him and his office that emerges in these pages; they shouldn't be this is a realistic snapshot of the decisive and visionary leader his colleagues have known and respected for decades.

President George H.W. Bush and his outstanding White House team were an inspiration for all of us who served his administration. Strong, principled and dedicated to putting America first regardless of the domestic political consequences, President Bush fully supported the National Space Council and me. He does not receive nearly the credit he deserves for successfully navigating one of the most perilous times in American history. Ronald Reagan certainly won the Cold War, George Bush won the peace. Do yourself a favor and read <u>A World Transformed</u>.

Finally, I owe a profound debt of gratitude to the men and women who served with me on the National Space Council staff. They not only brought to the Council extraordinary experience and knowledge, they demonstrated through their tireless service an extraordinary dedication to country. Each of them made unique and significant contributions to aspects of the national space program, but most importantly they made an enduring contribution to us all by ensuring that the President of the United States had timely, accurate and balanced information upon which to make important decisions about America's space program.

Many people helped translate my original manuscript into publishable English; starting with my wife who has made a career out of improving everything I do. T. Trent Gegax was an original co-conspirator in crafting the 'story line' of this work and gave me every opportunity to make the result a coherent and compelling story. I hope I succeeded to a small degree, thanks largely to Trent. Matteo Pangallo from UMass Amherst edited the document and was extremely helpful in identifying places where I abused and potentially confused a lay reader. I have tried to make adjustments for clarity and ease of understanding.

I have doubtless excluded others who have provided important support and made significant contributions to the book and the effort. It is unintentional. If you are reading this and are thinking, "Why am I not mentioned, I should be?" You are right, I apologize.

Above all, I owe an eternal debt of gratitude to Kathe Hicks Albrecht. She lived this journey as a partner, suffered my frustrations and doubts and always patted me on the back, provided encouraging words and perspectives and infused me with her sunny warmth, optimism and charity. To those who don't automatically associate me with these attributes I only ask you to consider what things would have been like without this wonderful and loving influence. Our children, Nicole, Alex and Olivia are living proof of her powerful and positive influence on people. Despite all this help and support, the resulting book is entirely my responsibility.

If nothing else, this book is a call for renewal and reinvigoration of American exceptionalism through our space exploration program. A significant part of that renewal will begin with the children of America who will always aim high. I hope this book can offer a lesson about who we were and are and can be. In this regard and in this spirit, I am dedicating the net proceeds of this book to the California State Summer School for Mathematics and Science (COSMOS). They have generously agreed to accept.

Mark Albrecht, January, 2011

TABLE OF CONTENTS

PART III

INTRODUCTION

"Are these the shadows of the things that Will be,
or are they shadows of things that May be, only?"
Charles Dickens, *A Christmas Carol*

*December 18, 1991 – Office of the Chief of Staff of the Vice President of the United
States, Old Executive Office Building (OEOB), the White House*

I arrived at the office of the Vice President's chief of staff on the third floor
of the Old EOB at 8:15am Thursday morning to participate in something
extraordinary. I was Executive Secretary of the White House National Space
Council, chaired by Vice President Dan Quayle, and we had asked for a face-
to-face meeting with three of the four living former NASA administrators to
elicit their collective judgment on the performance and tenure of the current
administrator, Admiral Richard H. Truly.

The Vice President's Chief of Staff, Bill Kristol was in a jocular mood
that morning and, as I entered his office, was on the phone with a prominent
reporter for the New York Times. Bill was commenting on a piece in that
morning's Washington Post written by E.J. Dionne and quoting Vice President
Quayle as saying Pat Buchanan's challenge to President Bush for the Republican nomination in 1992 was "out of step" with the conservative base of the
Republican party, especially when it came to foreign policy.[1] He laughed off
Quayle's defense of Dick Darman in the article and proceeded to offer that,
while Buchanan had the better case when it came to federal spending and taxes,
his rhetoric on foreign policy amounted to an isolationist and protectionist
platform that was "loony". He waved me in with a broad gesture that signified
his comfort and trust – something not to be taken for granted; after all, he was
consistently hounded by Bush loyalists as a "leaker", especially when it came to
dissension within the ranks regarding "moderate" Bush economic policies.

Bill hung up the phone and shook his head, "Buchanan shouldn't even be in the field of view, our economic policy is a disaster, and we have created an opening a mile wide. Fortunately, Pat uses all his fire on a far right isolationist foreign policy." Bill's secretary, Kathleen Connolly, had gone to the 17th Street entrance of the Old EOB to escort two distinguished looking retired executives to the ceremonial office suite of the Vice President on the third floor. Her maiden name is Buchanan; she is Pat's sister.

In a matter of minutes, Kathleen returned and said, "The two gentlemen are here. Shall I try to get Mr. Fletcher on the phone?" Bill nodded, and as she turned, in walked the former administrators.

Jim Beggs was a tall, thin man in his mid-sixties at the time, with a shock of white hair. He had been the 6th NASA administrator, serving in the early Reagan administration. He ambled, slightly hunched over, to the large desk behind which Kristol sat and shook hands. Beggs retired to an armchair and draped his large frame rather casually over the leather seat.

Tom Paine had just turned seventy had served as the 3rd NASA administrator, taking over from the legendary James Webb and serving during the short but critical period from 1969 -1970. Paine, a shorter and stockier man than Beggs, but with a more earnest and forthright style, exchanged greetings and sat next to me. Only Bob Frosch, who served as NASA administrator under Carter, and James Fletcher, who served twice, under Nixon and later Reagan, were absent. Frosch was on unavoidable travel; Fletcher lay on his deathbed.

Kristol thanked the two former administrators for their patience as the topic of the day's meeting had been somewhat vague. Now he was direct and clear. NASA had a vacancy in the Deputy Director position. J.R. Thompson, former director of the Marshall Space Flight Center in Huntsville, Alabama, had vacated the post three months earlier, for no apparent reason. Bill explained that we were having a difficult time recruiting a replacement for J.R. and were consistently hearing from otherwise promising candidates that they would not work for Dick Truly. Were Beggs and Paine were aware of this?

Beggs spoke first, in a slow, western Pennsylvania drawl. "I'm aware of the difficulties in finding a suitable Deputy at NASA. It will be difficult to get an outside candidate for this position because of the space and industrial community's widespread concerns with the competence of current senior management at NASA."

Paine agreed and said, "It is common knowledge that J.R. has resigned in large measure because of his dissatisfaction with NASA management."

Kristol dryly observed that there is only one *layer* of management above the Deputy Administrator: Admiral Truly. He asked directly, "What is your assessment of Dick Truly?"

Paine responded in his distinctive, hoarse voice. "Dick Truly is a fine man and good astronaut, but he is simply over his head as NASA administrator. Like so many astronauts, Dick has inadequate experience as a senior manager and fills far too many senior positions with individuals that have similar backgrounds to his own, and a similar lack of management experience."

Beggs, warming to the task added, "Truly has insulated and isolated himself and has developed a 'bunker mentality', avoiding negative feedback and missing important opportunities to improve things by making needed changes in programs and organization."

Kristol pressed the case. "Is Dick Truly the right man for NASA? Do we need to make a change?"

"No he isn't", said Beggs, "You need new leadership."

"Look, Dick Truly has been given multiple opportunities to adapt and grow in the job and, regrettably, he has failed to do so," added Paine. "At this point, NASA needs a change, the country needs a change. We are at a critical point in America's space program, perhaps America's entire future. We won the Cold War, but are now faced with something possibly even more challenging: the victory. President Bush has done all that we could ask of him: he has recognized the pivotal importance of space to America's future economic health, he has focused resources on the problem, he has given clear direction and rationale for a vibrant space program after the Cold War. But most of all, he has expended precious political capital in turbulent times in order to keep America exploring, innovating and pressing ahead. The window is open, but it will not be open forever, perhaps not even much longer. NASA has simply flunked the course, pulled in its head, and buckled to the worst parochial instincts of its research centers. And in my book, the buck stops with the administrator."

Each of us paused. Paine had said it all. At that moment, Kathleen opened the door. "Mrs. Fletcher says Mr. Fletcher is on the line, but it will be a moment before he can sit up and talk." Jim Fletcher was home, in bed, dying of lung cancer at 72.   Fletcher would die four days later. Weak and frail and barely able to talk, he whispered into the line, "Tom is absolutely correct. Dick is a fine man, but needs to step aside so that we can have a chance to make a new start." The die was cast.

Bill Kristol thanked Fletcher, Beggs, and Paine for their candor and obvious commitment to America and its space program. He added that the administration would not take any action lightly, but that, indeed, "the stakes here are high – very high." He asked them to keep this conversation confidential and said that we would share their thoughts with the Vice President and the President.

Two months later, on February 10, 1992, Dick Truly resigned as NASA administrator.

We assumed that a change of command at NASA would result in a change in direction for the civil space program. But while a change at the top was a necessary condition, it proved to be insufficient. The forces that had effectively ground our civil space program to a halt were much more powerful than one or two leaders at the top of the agency. As we were to learn over the next decade, even with courageous and visionary leadership, even with vigorous support and leadership from the White House, the end of the Cold War effectively ended the US human space exploration program. Some argue that it began a period of decline in the United States.

———

Today there is a vigorous debate about whether America is in fact in decline. Are our best days are behind us? Will our children grow up in an America with more opportunity or less? With more education or less? In a nation that leads or a nation that follows?

Surely claims of America in decline are, at most, premature. Nevertheless, decline is a *possible* future path for America. The Great Space Race and the space exploration that the United States pursued as a central part of that

race were critical elements in America's success in the latter half of the twentieth century. We explored space not only because of our competition with the
Soviet Union in ideas and technology and military force, but because we were
optimistic about the future. Our future. We explored space to enrich our lives
and empower our people. Space exploration did enrich and empower us, and
propelled us to prominence among nations. Space exploration has kept us safe
and improved our lives and exploration has lead inevitably to a better future.
But the simple fact is that, as the Cold War ended, we stopped exploring. We
didn't do it all at once, but we stopped nevertheless.

So why on earth did we stop?

This book is a firsthand account of how the United States effectively abandoned its space exploration program after it won the Cold War. There is no
one cause, no one interest or actor responsible, but there are clear and important influences that contributed to the result. Our institutions became bloated,
wasteful, and bureaucratic. Elected representatives became fiscal stewards of
jobs in their states and districts, making efficient and coherent allocation of
resources nearly impossible. Private industry learned to wield its consolidated
power to smother competition, grow cost, and mimic its slow and bureaucratic
customer. And the academic community, for its part, learned to deftly use its
power to influence, adjudicate, and validate government science initiatives in
order to ensure that it got its "fair share" of the exploration pie. It is often said
that the Pentagon is an iron triangle of industry, the Congress and the military
services. In fact, the civil space program is a steel quadrangle of industry, Congress, the NASA bureaucracy, and academic scientists. In end, there was little
left of what was once the crown jewel of the age of American exceptionalism.

For their part, the Russians abandoned their human space exploration program more quickly and quietly than did the United States. The economic
rigors of the Cold War defeat and the radical restructure of their institutions
and economy in the 1990's compelled Russia to emphasize harvesting space
technology for short term cash rather than investing in pushing new horizons.
We could see the beginnings the demise of the Russian space program at the
end stages of the Cold War. Our hope was to channel their need for immediate economic return into cooperative human space exploration activities with
the United States. What we feared and urgently attempted to prevent was the

rogue marketing of space technology to new aspirants for power and prestige in a 'post Cold War' world. On net, this effort has been a qualified success.

At the end of the day, both the United States and Russia resigned from the Great Space Race we had created and America had won.

———

Except where noted, all material for this book comes from my personal notes and records of meetings and conversations, and from public documents available at the George H.W. Bush Presidential Library on the campus of Texas A&M University. All errors of fact and judgment are mine and mine alone.

I.

THE CALL

It was Friday afternoon on February 24, 1989. Cynthia Furneau, longtime administrative assistant to Congressman, then U.S. Senator, and newly sworn in Vice President Dan Quayle called me at my desk in Senator Pete Wilson's office, where I had spent the last six years as the senator's advisor on national security affairs. It was a call I had been waiting for. "Dan would like you to come down to the White House to see him first thing Monday morning."

I had previously met with the newly elected, but yet to be sworn in Vice President earlier in January, 1989 when he was temporarily camped in an office in Lafayette Square, across from the White House. I had met with him for lunch in this small "transition" office and waded my way through the little spaces, passed Cynthia Furneau, and Quayle's newly appointed Press Secretary, Dave Beckwith. Beckwith was a former political reporter for Time magazine specializing in the Supreme Court and, lately, the 1988 campaign. Dave is a tall man with sandy red hair and, at the time, a Herman Melville beard covering his chin and chops, but with no moustache. He looked like a turn of the century Bostonian. Bob Guttman greeted me at the office door. Guttman a Senate veteran and Quayle's staff assistant on the Labor and Education subcommittee, was now the incoming Vice President's chief of staff. I always thought Bob was an odd choice for chief of staff. He was certainly sufficiently smart and savvy for the job, but he was more the quiet "academic" type than a political operative and he seemed a little senior and frail for Dan Quayle, who was young, energetic, and very political. And given the unprecedented and

savage campaign Quayle had endured in 1988, I expected him to have staffed
a political team aimed to reestablishing himself as the up and coming future
of the Republican Party. By the time he was four months into the job, he did
just that by moving Bill Kristol into the chief of staff's position and Spence
Abraham into the domestic policy job vacated by Bill. Within a year, Quayle
was to build a first class political and policy team that was widely recognized
for excellence, though only grudgingly by a press corps that stubbornly resisted
a reevaluation of the Quayle caricature created in the 1988 campaign.

When I met with Dan Quayle in his transition offices that day in January 1989, we hadn't seen each other since the Republican Convention in New
Orleans the previous summer, before the campaign and before his nomination
to be George Bush's running mate. Seeing Quayle that day in January brought
instantly to mind memories of the convention and the battles that were fought
over the contents of the party platform. I had worked on the convention's
platform committee as the staff director of the National Security and Foreign
Policy subcommittee that had been chaired by Bay Buchanan, Pat's sister and
former Treasurer of the United States under Ronald Reagan and New Orleans
Congressman Bob Livingstone (later to become, however briefly, Speaker of
the House of Representatives). We had a draft National Security and Foreign Policy plank of the platform when we went to New Orleans – a plank
that I had helped write and that had been "blessed" by the Bush team led by
Brent Scowcroft. Most of the content of the platform was easily agreed upon,
including Republican standards such as "peace through strength", "modernized strategic forces and the MX missile", and "an all volunteer force". But it
also included carefully crafted words on strategic defenses and President Reagan's Strategic Defense Initiative (SDI). I was disappointed with the negotiated
wording of the draft as it was very cautious and passive regarding SDI, relying
heavily on an "arms control" community consensus on the matter and stating
that SDI was a research program to be strictly limited and used primarily as
a counterbalance for additional and more advantageous offensive arms limits
in a "grand bargain". The draft language supported "research exclusively to
evaluate the feasibility of strategic defenses". Implicitly, nothing was to be done
that might provide a basis or plan for actual deployments. The research was
to be undertaken strictly within the provisions of the Anti-Ballistic Missile

(ABM) Treaty, consistent with the "narrow" interpretation of the treaty itself with regard to "exotic technologies (like lasers and directed energy weapons)". It was clear that no broadening of the treaty was to be allowed and any future deployments would be subject to the highest bars of demonstrated technical feasibility and affordability, as well as a new criterion: "cost effectiveness on the margin". With the testing limitations implicitly dictated in such a "treaty compliant" research program, there was almost no possibility for defenses to become a reality. It was a dead end street. Research forever — deployment never. This was dictated from on high by Brent and I was clearly instructed to "keep the committee in the box" on the issue.

Neither Buchanan nor Livingstone was happy with the language on SDI and they asked whether the committee could "amend" and "improve" it. We had several sidebars with Brent and Senator John Tower, who also was part of the "oversight" committee of the campaign. Bay Buchanan and Bob Livingstone argued strongly that SDI was a political winner and that George Bush should enthusiastically support, not undercut, Ronald Reagan's initiative. They argued that the initiative made perfect sense, provided positive hope for the American public, and was clearly pushing the Soviets to the breaking point. Brent, however, argued that the language would send the wrong signal about the Bush administration's intentions, would back the Soviets into a dangerous corner, and that the committee shouldn't tie the new President's hands. He offered a reassurance of the Vice President's support and commitment to SDI, but it lacked the ring of conviction behind it and the committee chairs were unimpressed. If anything, they left these meetings more convinced than ever that strong platform language was necessary to keep SDI from becoming a "bargaining chip" for additional offensive arms agreements in the Bush administration.

I was asked to draft amended SDI language for the platform — language that would be more forward-leaning and based on the assumption that, should strategic defenses prove feasible, affordable, and stable in managing offensive countermeasures, the United States would pursue deployments utilizing the mechanisms that existed in the ABM Treaty, including potentially resigning from the treaty altogether. The amendment was drafted, offered by a committee member from Nebraska, and passed unanimously. At the time, joining a potential Bush administration as a senior official was the farthest thing from my mind and pushing back on the Bush convention leadership team on this topic seemed like a principled stand. As it turned out, Brent was neither to forget that amendment to the platform, nor the staffer who assisted in its creation.

———

Nevertheless, five months later on that January day in 1989, Vice President-elect Dan Quayle and I had a sandwich and reminisced about this, and about the incredible journey he had travelled since New Orleans. And although he was characteristically sunny and positive, I could tell that he was still simmering over the entire campaign – from the awkward and ill prepared announcement, to the assignment of and his subordination to handlers, to the friction inside the campaign. He clearly felt that the tight control to which he had been subjected was in neither his nor the campaign's best interests and was a set-up for a controversial Vice Presidency. Quayle is a remarkable person. Never once did he express or reveal anger or outrage at the process that would forever mark him, unfairly as it is, as "damaged goods".

We soon got down to business and Quayle said he was considering me for one of two assignments: his National Security Advisor, or, Executive Secretary of a new White House National Space Council that he was to chair. I didn't need to think about that for a moment. I wanted to be the National Security Advisor to the Vice President of the United States. Quayle understood my position and asked that I give serious thought to both. He said that, for the Space Council position, he was also considering Hank Cooper, at that time chief negotiator for the United States at the Defense and Space Talks in Geneva and formerly the Deputy at the Arms Control and Disarmament Agency – but there were some reports coming from Geneva that were potentially troubling… but he didn't elaborate. I also asked about my friend, and Quayle's current National Security assistant, Henry Sokolski, saying that I didn't want to compete with Henry if he was in the running for the Security Advisor's job. Quayle assured me that Henry was *not* a candidate for the National Security job so I shouldn't feel as though I was competing with a friend or pushing him aside for my own advancement. As I departed Lafayette Square that day headed back to my office on Capitol Hill, I began to seriously contemplate what it would mean to join the administration as a member of the White House staff and who might support and who might oppose my nomination. As soon as I got back to the Senate I called Henry and told him about my meeting with his boss. He was genuinely appreciative and said he really didn't know what was going on.

Then I waited… for what seemed an eternity, but was actually less than thirty days. Finally, Cynthia's call came that Friday in February and I was as curious as I was anxious about what the Vice President had on his mind. And I had the weekend to think about it.

II.

"WELCOME TO THE NFL!"

Vince Lombardi

I had been to the White House many times before, but my visit on this gray, damp Monday morning was different. I was provided a spot in the coveted West Wing parking lot between the West Wing and the Old Executive Office building. I was badged at the street entrance to the West Wing on 'E' Street rather than the usual OEOB visitor entrance on 17th Street and, after proceeding past the guard shack, I parked just a few steps from the awning of the West Wing's "VIP" entrance, the one through which cabinet officials and senior advisors are often seen scurrying during some crisis. It is the "working" entrance to the West Wing, as opposed to the "formal" entrance in the front, where newscasters and post-visit press availabilities with Congressional leaders are routinely held.

Cynthia was inside the automatic doors to the West Wing, all smiles and ready with a warm hug. She showed me around the basement floor, the White House mess, and some of the offices. The walls were full of large, framed photos of the President and Vice President at recent events or on trips. She told me that these "jumbos" were changed every week or two to reflect the current activities of the President.

We walked up the back stairs, just off the basement entrance to the West Wing, to the main level of the building. The halls seemed very small; in fact, the entire West Wing struck me as rather small and constricted. A couple of turns around corners past more "jumbos" and cramped offices and there we were in the outer office of the Vice President's West Wing office. This was Cynthia's turf and, while tastefully appointed in impeccable Federalist style, there were plenty of personal items and grandmotherly mementos arrayed on her desk and credenza.

Shortly, the door to the office opened and several people emerged still talking at the end of what had obviously been a business meeting between staff and principal. And there was the Vice President of the United States. "Doc! How are you doing? What took you so long to visit?" This was vintage Quayle: a disarming, warm greeting with a little twist of irony.

The office was magnificent and, unlike the warrens and tight hallways in the West Wing, the room was large. It was divided into two parts. In front, near the entrance, there was a living room seating area centered around a large fireplace, with a love seat and two upholstered club chairs at either end of a nautical looking coffee table. Toward the rear of the room was a large desk surrounded by formal chairs – clearly just occupied by those who were leaving the office as I arrived. The walls were decorated with numerous paintings, from portraits to landscapes, all museum quality, distinctly American, and 19th century vintage. There was a credenza behind the Vice President's desk and numerous items of memorabilia were on display, including photos of Marilyn, the children, and the family.

We sat by the fireplace, the Vice President in the club chair with his left arm draped across the top and I somewhat awkwardly on the love seat. Cynthia asked if we wanted anything to drink; we didn't, and so we started.

"How have you been? You taking care of Wilson and my friends in the Senate? Golly, the place has gone to pot since I left. What are you doing up there?" We chatted briefly about matters before the Senate and the activities of the Armed Services Committee, now under the leadership of Democrat Sam Nunn from Georgia. We quickly turned to the nomination of Senator John Tower to be Secretary of Defense. Quayle was a friend of Tower's and strongly supported his nomination by President Bush. The President had announced the nomination of Tower early in December and the Senate as a matter of course, referred it to the Armed Services Committee for urgent consideration. Within weeks leaks began to appear in the press that there were "problems with the nomination." The leaks were salacious, compelling, and anonymous. By February the nomination had finally progressed to a vote in the committee for recommendation to the full Senate.

I told the Vice President that I was in the room when the Armed Services Committee vote on Tower took place the previous Thursday evening, on February 23. The Vice President leaned forward and eagerly asked that I recount every detail. I described the tension in the air that night and the solemnity of the roll call vote. I told him that, before the vote, Senator Warner believed that we would leave the committee deadlocked, 10 – 10, with assurances made to Senator John McCain (R-AZ) that Senator Richard Shelby (D-AL) would break ranks with his Democratic colleagues and vote "aye" for the nomination. After all, Warner reasoned, Chairman Nunn had said time and again that this was not a partisan matter, but rather a matter of conscience for each member to resolve individually. And, characteristically, Senator Warner believed him.

Senator Nunn had elected to conduct the vote in the large committee room of the Commerce Committee, in the Dirksen Office Building, rather than in the smaller Senate Armed Services committee room in the Russell Building because of the controversy regarding the nomination and ensuing public attention. This room is a cavernous art deco homage to American power right out of an Ayn Rand novel. Large statues in heroic poses grace the marble walls and enormous brass sconces look as if fires should be burning in them as they flank the large and lofty carved wooden dais. It was a fitting venue for the final argumentation and jury vote in what was essentially a trial. As with most committee and caucus rooms in the Senate office buildings, there is an antechamber just behind the center chair on the dais. This antechamber has separate access to the hallway and is used by committee members both as their private access and exit from the chamber itself and as a small meeting room to conduct private discussions. In fact, Senator Wilson and I had entered through the antechamber as we proceeded to the caucus room itself that evening. As we passed through the anteroom, I saw Senators Levin and Nunn and their staffs huddling and speaking softly. Uncharacteristically, there was little chatter as the senators arrived and took their seats. Faces were drawn and extremely serious, the air thick with anticipation and electricity.

Senator Nunn gaveled the committee to order and stated the meeting's purpose "to make a recommendation to the Senate on whether President Bush's nominee for the Secretary of Defense, John Tower, should be confirmed for this high position."[2] Nunn spoke briefly about the difficulty of this decision; he praised Senator Tower for his service and recognized his contribution to the work of the committee, his patriotism, and devotion to country. "John Tower is a loyal, patriotic American, who has a solid record of public service…dedicated to our Nation's security." Nunn reiterated his stated position of impartiality: "We on this committee have made no rush to judgment. I believe that every member has approached this task with a sincere effort to vote in the best interests of our Nation. I believe that about members on both sides of the aisle."

Then Nunn began his lengthy dissection of the nomination, starting with the high standards for nomination qualifications and candidate characteristics set impartially by the committee before the election. He then proceeded to slowly enumerate the charges against Tower and the implications for his discharge of the office. There were allegations of alcohol abuse, others regarding relationships with women, still more regarding conflicts of interest stemming from his work as a consultant for defense contractors. Each charge was explored and diagnosed and the evidence weighed. In the end Nunn said, "I am skeptical as to the nominee's ability to restore public trust in Pentagon management. I am concerned as to his ability to command the confidence and respect of his subordinates and to set the moral standards for the men and women in uniform. I cannot in good conscience vote to put an individual at the top of the chain of command when his history of excessive drinking is such that he would not be selected to command a missile wing or Strategic Air Command bomber squadron."

At earlier meetings on the nomination, Nunn had said that, had President Bush appointed Senator Tower to be his National Security Advisor, he would not have raised an objection, but because of the statutory authority for command delegated uniquely to the Secretary of Defense, he was compelled to vote against the Tower nomination. Therefore, he concluded, "with considerable reluctance, but with a clear conscience, I will vote 'no' on the Tower nomination."

The entire room was silent. Senator Nunn yielded to Senator Warner, who thanked the chair and congratulated him on how "fair and objective" he had been in the review of this nomination and how he, Warner, had been "accorded...a full partnership in performing those steps that have brought us to this historic moment in this hearing." By mutual agreement between Nunn and Warner, the committee's action on the nomination had been delayed on several occasions so that new allegations could be investigated. Nunn even alluded to this in his opening remarks: "We have made no rush to judgment.... Additional inquiries have been ordered by the FBI as late as last night on recent allegations received by the committee."

Warner said that, while he respected the Chairman's position on this matter, "we part at this juncture, for I cast my vote for John Tower," and he proceeded to offer a strong defense of Senator Tower and his candidacy as the President's choice to be Secretary of Defense. In turn, each Senator, first Democrat and then Republican, read carefully prepared statements, each side generally repeating the same set of arguments: for the Democrats, that Tower's alleged drinking, his relationships with women and defense contractors, in the words of Senator Levin (D-MI), "fall unacceptably short" of the kind of behavior required of "the number two person in the chain of command and a person who must lead the Pentagon through an exceedingly difficult period"; for the Republicans the case was one of anonymous, unjust, and suspect innuendo and rumor balanced against the firsthand knowledge and witness of colleagues, coworkers, and, in particular, the President of the United States himself. Senator Cohen likened the "experience of John Tower as a nominee for Secretary of Defense" to the gruesome image of the charred, swinging bodies of "two people shot, hanged, and then set afire" in the TV miniseries based on the Larry McMurtry novel of the Old West, *Lonesome Dove*.

Senator Wilson said, "In this instance, the confirmation process has been hijacked and corrupted. Anonymous leaks to the network evening news have unfairly and falsely depicted John Tower to be unfit to be Secretary of Defense because of allegations of personal problems."

Senator McCain expressed incredulity that the fulsome and public praise lavished on Senator Tower by the committee members he had known, traveled with, and worked with over the years could be apparently swept aside by anony-

mous and false charges by strangers. He said, "I will presume all the praise
heaped on Senator Tower during all of these years was sincere. I am very curious, as I think the American people should be: why has there been this incredible change of opinion over these last two months?"

Remarkably, the specific and heated charges of hypocrisy, corruption, and
character assassination by leaked rumor, double hearsay, and inspired innuendo were being lodged against the very people in that room. No one outside
of the FBI had access to the allegations and investigations regarding the nomination — except for the Senators and their staffs assembled in that room that
night...and everyone knew it. I had seen Senators time and again express outrage and umbrage at even the slightest suggestion of partisanship or hypocrisy
on the floor of the Senate and in committee — sometimes very nearly coming to
blows — and yet that night all the Democrats sat motionless and expressionless,
like they were participating in a show trial. There were even suggestions that
Senator Jim Exon (D-NE) was actually inebriated that evening. And remarkably, as well, none of the discussion addressed a single item of national security
policy. Not one. Senators went on at length on these two lines of argument.
Senator Cohen alone filled the record with thousands of words of argument for
Tower and against a process seized by rumor and innuendo with not a "shred
of credible evidence."

Senator Richard Shelby, who sat at the end of the long line of committee
Democrats, was the last to speak. He looked distinctly uncomfortable as he
read his prepared text of less than 200 words and announced that, in his judgment, "the nomination was crippled beyond repair" and that he would oppose
the nomination. We were stunned.

The clerk called the roll alphabetically, and then it came to Shelby. "Senator Shelby?" asked the clerk. "No," was the reply. An audible gasp erupted
from the Republican side of the table. The clerk finished the roll call and then
announced the committee's decision: "the motion to report the nomination
favorably is not agreed to."

Senator Nunn then delivered the *coup de grâce*: "I now move that the nomination of John Tower be reported *unfavorably*, with the recommendation that the
nomination not be confirmed by the Senate." A chance, a fig leaf perhaps for
those whose conscience was burdened by the process, to abstain or vote present —

but it was not to be. The fix was in and Chairman Nunn already knew the outcome. The roll was called again and, again, 11 to 9: "The motion that the nomination be reported unfavorably, with the recommendation that the nomination not be confirmed by the Senate is approved." It was 9:00pm and, like an execution, it was over.

As Senator Thad Cochran was later to say, "It is hard to believe that twenty Senators, exposed to the exact same information about a candidate and under the injunction to make up their minds solely based on their conscience and judgment, would split 11 to 9 exactly along party lines."

So much for the Chairman's oft-stated position that each Senator was to decide the matter based on the merits and their personal judgment, without regard to party loyalty. And so much for Senator Warner's strategy to avoid confronting the Chairman and pressing for action while ever more frivolous and ludicrous allegations rolled up on Senator Tower, in the hopes that this "indulgence" would keep Nunn from becoming partisan.

The meeting was quickly gaveled to a close and Shelby, at the far end of the table, literally bolted for the antechamber door. The way was crowded as Senators stood from their chairs to talk and gather their materials, and so Shelby's progress to the door was impeded. I had left through the antechamber door and was standing with other staff members in the anteroom, looking at each other in disbelief as to what had just happened, when in through the door burst Senator McCain, absolutely fuming. He stormed in and started a tirade. This was interrupted shortly by the entrance into the room of Senator Shelby.

Senator Shelby is a large but not physically imposing man. He is almost 6' 4" tall, with a trim, athletic build, a gentle demeanor, and a soft Alabama accent. Without hesitation, Senator McCain lunged at Senator Shelby. Shelby looked like an adolescent in the grips of the junior high school vice principal. "I couldn't go against the Chairman, John."

Quayle hated the outcome, but was intensely interested in the story. He agreed that Shelby had performed shamelessly, that Nunn had exacted revenge on Tower, and that, as on so many other occasions, Senator Warner had been completely outmaneuvered, outgunned, and outfoxed by Senator Nunn. He said they still had hopes to turn a few votes on the floor, but the performance in committee sent a clear signal that the Democrats were willing to go to the mat on this issue. He wasn't sure if the President was.

Not a day after I had met with the Vice President, George Bush, on his way back to Washington from the funeral of the emperor in Japan, signaled that while he wouldn't budge an iota on the candidacy of John Tower, he didn't want to make this a confrontation with the Congress. Tower was sunk.

I told Quayle that after the vote on Tower, I was sitting next to Senator Bill Cohen (R-ME) in the small underground tram that ran between the Hart Senate Office Building and the Capitol. I congratulated him on his defense of Tower and his willingness to stand up to the process publically. I told Cohen that I had worked in the Senate for six years, and every day I felt that if any citizen had been party to everything I had seen and heard, they would be proud of the institution and the people who served them. But that day I was ashamed, and I believe any honest citizen would be ashamed of what had happened. And Senator Cohen simply nodded his head in agreement. The Vice President sat momentarily in stunned silence looking out on the front lawn of the White House.

After a few moments, Quayle turned to the real purpose of our meeting. He said, "Albrecht, I want you to run the National Space Council for me." I was shocked. What happened to the National Security Advisor job, I wondered? What happened to Hank Cooper, who was clearly more qualified for the space job? What on earth *was* this job and what on earth would I do with it? All these thoughts ran through my mind. I think I blurted out, "OK."

He proceeded to tell me that Congress had directed that the President form a National Space Council and that the Vice President chair it. He said that the President had decided to comply with this authorization and planned to issue a Presidential directive to implement it.[3] Quayle explained that I would be appointed by the President and part of the President's staff, but that as a practical matter, I would report to him. Cynthia would take me upstairs to the head of White House Personnel to start the lengthy process of disclosing the background information and data necessary for my "full field" FBI investigation.

I asked about the National Security post and he said, "Do you know Carry Lord?" I had heard of Carnes Lord, but didn't know him well. Quayle said, "I discussed the matter with Brent and proposed a couple of candidates and he recommended Lord." I could tell there was more to the story.

"Did Brent say anything about me?"

"Actually he did. He said he didn't know you well but remembered you from New Orleans and the platform committee. He said Carnes would be a stronger candidate, but that he had no objections to you in the Space Council job." I knew immediately that he recalled the SDI amendment I had helped draft and the work of the National Security and Foreign Policy subcommittee. I had probably lost the National Security Advisor post as a consequence of those days in New Orleans, but I still took comfort in thinking that maybe, just maybe, Bush had won because of his strong positions on national security, including his strong, if somewhat coerced, support of SDI.

I had to ask about Hank Cooper. Quayle told me that during the preparation and processing of the Tower nomination, an article in Playboy magazine savaged the entire US Defense and Space delegation in Geneva for being a virtual bacchanal. Sordid details of personal relationships, non-stop partying, and unseemly conduct proved to be the source of many of the rumors and innuendo about Tower, as he had been head of that delegation. His replacement upon retirement was Hank Cooper. And while there were no specific allegations against Hank – and while both Quayle and I knew Hank and his wife, Bobby, very well and knew without question that Hank was the soul of probity – it was also clear that the Bush administration didn't need more high profile appointments associated with the Defense and Space delegation in Geneva. Hank is a terrific and talented man who shortly thereafter was appointed to lead the Strategic Defense Initiative office under the newly confirmed Secretary of Defense, Dick Cheney.

And so it was on March 1, 1989, that the President announced his intention to nominate me as the Executive Director of the National Space Council. I went to work the following week.

Response to my appointment was cautious but generally positive. The Gannett News Service reported on March 3, "Albrecht is an expert on national security [and] is known as a quick study." They continued, "Some aerospace experts – noting that Albrecht, like Quayle, has expertise in military space – expressed fear that NASA might take a back seat to the Pentagon in future policy decisions because of Albrecht's military intelligence background."[4]

Later, Bruce Reed, a speechwriter for Senator Al Gore, described me in the *New Republic* as "a space hawk" and predicted that the Space Council would make "militarization of outer space as more or less inevitable."[5]

The Economist noted, "The biggest challenge facing Albrecht, congressional aides say, will be to negotiate peace and find common ground among the competing interests of the space panel. One former congressional aide says: 'Albrecht is very bright, very competent, but nothing can prepare you for that sort of work. It's like war.'"[6]

And, in the manner of a "Welcome to the NFL" sign from the Washington media, there was a small item in a trade publication, *Satellite Week*, that noted somewhat snidely, though nevertheless accurately, "Albrecht won the job over what was rumored as sure shoe-in Henry Cooper, former arms control negotiator. Sources said his name was withdrawn from consideration because of 'alleged' close ties to embattled Defense Secretary-designate, John Tower."[7] I would learn very quickly that, in Washington, the difference between being the staff and being the principal was enormous.

III.

MY FIRST MISTAKE

"Fool me once, shame on you, fool me twice. . .shame on me"

The White House is not the monolith that it appears to be from the outside. Start with the matter of badges: there are three associated with White House access. There is the blue-edged badge, which is the equivalent of the "all access" pass to the White House, the West Wing, the Old EOB, and the "New EOB" just up the street at 17th and Eye Streets. Then there is the orange badge, which signifies Executive Office of the President status, but limits the holder to the New and Old EOBs. Entrance to the West Wing and the White House itself is prohibited without "blue badge" escort. Other visitors to the White House are issued the characteristic pink badge with a large "A" in the center signifying visitor status and also indicating that the individual was not to be left alone on the premises.

For cabinet secretary deputies, agency heads, ambassadors, and others, actual White House badges signify a degree of "closeness" to the administration. It was always interesting to watch senior officials look at each others' badges as they waited for White House meetings... one with a coveted "blue badge" another with the dreaded "A" badge. White House senior staff were constantly asked by the senior staff of agency and department heads to get their bosses White House badges so that they could avoid the time consuming and inefficient wait for "badging" at the gates. We all knew this was part of the game. And, of course, there's the ultimate cache: no badge at all. This luxury is afforded only the most senior staff and cabinet secretaries who are "face recognized" by the Secret Service.

My first few weeks in the White House were consumed with setting up a new office, hiring new staff, working with the Office of Management and Budget (OMB) to establish a budget, acquiring office equipment, meeting and introducing myself to both the White House team members and those in the space community that were the stakeholders, participants, and department and agency leads in executing the national space program. Days were hectic and long. Very long. Everyone wanted to introduce himself or herself and make a firsthand assessment of both me and the new organization.

I recall my first day. I was "processed" in the New EOB up the street and received the coveted blue badge and even more coveted parking space in Lafayette Square, right across from the White House. I entered the Old Executive Office Building (OEOB) from the 17th Street entrance and proceeded to the fourth floor, Room 420.

The OEOB is a phenomenal building, ornate and cavernous and, as a turn-of-the-century fire prevention measure, almost completely made of cast iron. I recall from the first visit how oddly quiet and empty the corridors seemed. Every door was shut. People spoke quietly as they earnestly paced down the large and dark corridors and the expansive staircases that form the center of the building. There are no windows in the interior hallways, no clocks… it was as if there was no such thing as time here, just the business of the government. It was an intimidating and imposing facility.

I entered Room 420 and found it empty except for a ramrod straight very tall Air Force colonel, who was seated in a solitary chair in the center of the room. He smiled broadly at my arrival. "Hello, I am Roger de Kok and I have been running the National Security Council Special Interagency Group (SIG) on space for the past six months. I think I work for you now." Roger was a terrific officer and good friend, and exactly the kind of "Indian guide" to the White House that I needed. He knew how to get things and how to get things done. We had one desk and a borrowed Wang word processor and printer from the NSC. Roger and I decided the first thing we needed to do was make stationery so that we could start communicating with the government and the space community. We talked about the National Space Council letterhead and quickly decided that we would avoid anything futuristic. Rather, we would go with a letterhead that communicated exactly the opposite: solidity, stability, and what we had the least of – tradition.

Unfortunately, Roger was already in transition to his new assignment in the Air Force and so his time with me was limited. His future in the Air Force was very bright. He eventually became a fine three-star Air Force general and a true visionary for the national security space program. The month I had with Roger was critically important for the entire enterprise. Many challenges that could have affected our clout and ultimately our utility to the President were overcome largely due to the wisdom, experience, and good will of Roger.

And challenges there were. Many apparently "small matters" were actually tests of the status and efficacy of the new White House Council. Everything from budgets to badges, furniture to phones, meeting lists to be included on to meetings that needed to be attended even without a formal invitation, were early tests of the status, power, and influence of the new organization, the Vice President,...and me.

Probably the most important of these tests came during an early visit from NASA's head of external affairs. His name is Ken Pedersen and he was a career NASA employee who had spent his entire time in headquarters working the NASA interfaces in Washington. Ken was trim, almost a slight, man with a superficially insouciant personality that belied a bureaucrat who was anything but detached. At times Ken seemed aloof, at others, dismissive. He clearly represented the institutional and "beltway" NASA that was none too pleased with the new Space Council.

Ken dropped by to introduce himself soon after we set up shop in mid-March. He chatted about this and that, probing about my views and on my plans for the Council. As he rose to leave he mentioned in an offhand manner that, among the pile of action items in my inbox, I would find a memo from him informing me that the NASA authorization bill that included authorization for the National Space Council also required the new administration to certify the President's support for the Space Station Freedom within 60 days of taking office.

"It is a simple and routine matter," said Ken. "I know you are busy so I have taken the liberty of drafting a response from the President to the Committee that simply states the obvious: namely that the President endorses the Space Station Freedom program." The response was due in one week.

As I was later to find, the request and the response was anything but routine. In the previous summer, Senator William Proxmire (D-WI), chairman of the Senate appropriation subcommittee on Housing and Urban Development (HUD), Veterans' Affairs (VA), and several independent agencies where the NASA budget resided, had essentially stopped NASA from proceeding with the Space Station Freedom out of concern about its cost and complexity. The request for an indication of Presidential support was specifically made in order to provide the administration an opportunity to "review, revise, or reject" the Space Station Freedom program *before* we became locked into it.

Regrettably, I did not address this matter with the focus and diligence it clearly required. I coordinated the response with the Vice President, OMB, the NSC, and the Office of Science and Technology Policy, all of whom were finding their new legs as well and couldn't imagine why we wouldn't make this certification. I visited my old friend and colleague Fred McClure, who had worked for Senator Tower and who now led the White House Office of Congressional Affairs, to discuss the matter. Within a day, on March 26, 1989, the letter affirming the President's commitment to the All American Space Station Freedom to be built entirely by space shuttle flights and on orbit assembly went out under the President's signature to the Committees on Science and Technology. Ironically, it was almost ten years and $40 billion dollars later when the Russian-built "Zarya" Functional Cargo Block – the first building element of the mightily downsized, no longer Freedom, but newly dubbed International Space Station (ISS) – was lifted into orbit from Baikonur, Kazakhstan on November 20, 1998 aboard a Russian Proton rocket.

It is arguable whether we could have in fact significantly impacted the Station project so early in the Bush administration by forcing a thorough review of cost and schedule and performance. Nevertheless, in retrospect I wish I had probed further, asked for relief on the deadline, and conducted a serious review. Regardless of the outcome, one thing would have been for sure - it would have hastened the impasse with NASA that was certainly to come.

IV.

"SOMETHING IS ROTTEN IN THE STATE OF DENMARK."

Shakespeare, *Hamlet*

By late April 1989 we were operating at a hectic pace, establishing an entirely new interagency coordination process and dealing with issues that were already surfacing, such as the disposition of the operational costs of the "Landsat" earth imaging satellite for wide area and multispectral mapping. Landsat is heavily used by the Interior and Agriculture departments for vegetation and geological research and land use management, and by the Department of Defense to generate maps used by major commands around the world. The recent change of administration created an opportunity for users of this "joint good" to back away from their portion of the Landsat operating costs in a financial game of chicken to see who would blink first and fill the gap... and to test the new Space Council. If the Council could not resolve this matter and enforce a funding plan apportioning cost across the departments and agencies quickly and successfully, then certainly more important and difficult policy and programmatic matters would elude our grasp and undermine out authority. The matter *was* resolved relatively quickly, and its significance was not lost on an attentive space community.

At the same time, we were beginning the process of interacting with the National Security Council, OMB, and other parts of the Executive Office of the President on day-to-day matters before the administration, including dealing with the various oversight committees on Capitol Hill that were analyzing and considering the President's first budget request. All the while, we were immersing ourselves in the detailed elements of the roughly $20 billion annual US space enterprise, as well as the numerous reports and recommendations for the President's consideration that had been produced during the previous year and were waiting for the Council to consider. Trade associations, committees on the Hill, individual members, and important national bodies such as the Space Science Board of the National Academies of Engineering and Science, all had important and thoughtful ideas and recommendations, and all needed to be digested and analyzed.

There were unclassified and routine defense space activities including space launch, telecommunications, weather, early warning, nuclear detonation detection, navigation, and mapping, and there were classified programs for global reconnaissance and intelligence gathering and the experimental and advanced programs of the Defense Advanced Research Projects Agency and the Strategic Defense Initiative Organization. We looked at the entire spectrum of requirements, from planning programs to execution. And of course we looked at the entire civil space program at NASA, with its extensive aeronautic and space science enterprises, including robotic planetary exploration, astronomy and astrophysics, huge wind tunnels and massive computer complexes to simulate and test new aero and astro design concepts, and a growing life sciences activity aimed at the other cornerstone of NASA: the human spaceflight program that was centered on the twin mega projects, the space shuttle and the Space Station Freedom.

It took very little time to come to two central observations about the state of the US space enterprise. First, defense and intelligence space programs were generally the result of disciplined processes of validated requirements from operational commands, tested and refined by a competitive internal resource allocation process overseen by a professional acquisition cadre, and finally adjudicated by the Joint Chiefs of Staff and civil authorities charged with executing specific, defined, and documented national security requirements. And second, by contrast, NASA was a jumble of activities that was a constant and dynamic balance of interests promoted and pursued by an active and vocal academic community, regional requirements based on a widely distributed "center" structure closely tied to local congressional delegations, the needs and demands of a large and growing astronaut corps, and a contractor community eager to unilaterally defend and expand individual ongoing activities. Finally there was what passed as the long term plans of NASA managers responsible for crafting a comprehensive and compelling program and vision that was to explain and weave together all of the above. At NASA, projects – like planets in our solar system – began as large collections of interests gradually coalescing around a kernel of activity, coalescing as each interest was slowly satisfied and so congealed into the larger "mission". As a consequence, projects were either miniscule one-offs to meet some need from a constituent interest unsatisfied by inclusion in a major program, or a major program itself – which by this time had become characteristically multibillion-dollar, decadal enterprises. As best as I could determine, these major projects were limited in cost, size, and schedule only by the capacity of the largest launch vehicle: the behemoth Titan IV. If we had had a heavier lifter, I am confident we would have had even more costly, bigger, and slower NASA projects.

The civil space program was lacking, and had lacked for some time, a consensus on long term, durable, and widely accepted goals.[8] I remarked to the Vice President in my first report on "the state of the space program," "You simply cannot find NASA in the constitution... [I]t is a completely discretionary activity and it is managed exactly as you would anticipate given that fact: namely, inefficiently, with lowest common denominator solutions that balance whole communities of stakeholders through compromise and program growth for the sole sake of consensus and some semblance of forward progress." The Space Station Freedom that we had recently certified to Congress was the most egregious example. It was, at the time, to be constructed with over seventeen dedicated space shuttle flights that were to include eight resupply and replenishment missions annually once it became partially manned five years after initial assembly. In other words, it would have more than three times the annual launch tempo ever achieved by the shuttle, with more astronaut extravehicular assembly hours than had been logged in the entire history of extravehicular activity...by all space fairing nations combined. The fact that this launch schedule was proposed as a baseline so soon after the Challenger accident in 1986 was, troubling. And though initially advertised to President Reagan six years earlier as an $8 billion cost, it was then estimated to cost over $30 billion. And it was growing.

"How do we get our arms around this?" asked the Vice President.

"I'm not sure, yet," I replied, "but two things seem obvious to me. First, NASA needs to resolve its multiple-masters dilemma by subordinating all stakeholders to a single baseline authority – not to disenfranchise them, but to subordinate them and their authority in terms of overall vision, requirements, plans and programs, and relative resource priority. While there is and can be joint responsibility and oversight, someone has to be in charge. You simply cannot have four or five hands on the wheel. And there can be only one solution to that problem, and that is that authority must be the President."

"Second, in order to establish that authority, we are going to have to exercise it and sustain it. NASA has no strategic vision, no compelling and central organizing mission to prioritize its plans and programs, and it doesn't have the clout to set or enforce them if it *could* prioritize them. They are a fantastic organization and represent a huge national capability, but they are floundering and need help - desperately."

"Get to work on it and give me a plan... soon," said Quayle.

Over the next several weeks I discussed these matters with members of the space community – people like Guy Stever, chairman of the National Academy of Engineering and author of the National Academy report, Congressman Bill Nelson of Florida, who had written the Vice President with recommendations about the space program, the heads of the Planetary Society and National Space Society, and current and former government and industry leaders.

But my first stop was to Richard G. Darman, the Director of the President's Office of Management and Budget. Darman was a long-term colleague of James Baker from Treasury and his roots in government went back to Elliot Richardson and the Nixon administration. He was a compact man with a wide grin and a quick biting wit. He was brilliant and somewhat eccentric, with a nearly encyclopedic knowledge of the federal budget, more than an amateur interest and intuition in political matters, and he was an absolute master of control; he worked longer and harder than anyone in the White House and would frequently tell anyone who would listen that he cut his own hair. I always wondered if it was because he wanted to save money, didn't trust anyone, or actually thought he did the job better than anyone else. I will let the result speak for itself.

Darman was also a space enthusiast. He liked the big and the bold, and the limitless boundaries of space. I believe he instinctively sensed that the agency was adrift and in need of control and readily agreed with my diagnosis of the situation at NASA and the need for action. Before I could even finish my analysis, Darman interrupted and said, "What NASA needs is a central organizing mission, an overriding objective that will provide the basis for rationalizing the entire enterprise and bring discipline to its management. And it's your job to help us find that!"

I also consulted with members of the broader space community, from industry, the science community, and those on the Hill – people I knew and whose opinions I trusted. To a person, they agreed with the general assessment of NASA and the need for change – substantial change.

Although many advisory reports and many private advisory recommendations had recently been put forth, none was more comprehensive, or more representative of the collective net assessment of the civil space program than the National Academy report.

This report clearly, succinctly, and pointedly addressed the status and needs of the civil space program. It called for clear leadership from the President in establishing and building a consensus on long term and durable goals for space, including forming an aggressive program of international cooperation, defining and supporting a stable level of federal funding that would emphasize a balanced base and new initiatives, choosing a strong NASA administrator to be part of the President's team, streamlining and revitalizing NASA management, and harmonizing activities between the Department of Defense and NASA to reduce cost, share innovative technologies, and create positive sum enterprises.

During this period the nomination of Richard Truly to be NASA's administrator was working its way through the committee process. Truly was a bona fide American hero. Astronaut, test pilot, co-pilot with Bob Crippen of the first Space Shuttle flight, lead investigator in the Challenger accident investigation, responsible for the "Return to Flight" Mission, and currently Chief of NASA Spaceflight Operations. I had met Truly only briefly when the Vice President and I were on a trip to Ohio for a Vice Presidential address on the US's economic competitiveness. President Bush's Chief of Staff, John Sununu, had told me before we left on that trip that the President intended to nominate Truly to be NASA administrator and wanted to make sure neither the Vice President nor I had any objection to the appointment. Neither of us knew or had an opinion about Truly and therefore had no objection, but I thought it would be essential, in the Vice President's new capacity, that he interview Truly before the announcement was made. We arranged for Truly to come onboard Air Force Two in Cleveland, so he and Quayle could spend a few minutes together.

Air Force Two at the time was a rotation of one of two former 707 Air Force Ones that, in the final days of the Reagan administration, had been replaced with a new 747 fleet. On this day we were flying tail number Special Air Mission (SAM) 26000 – the airplane that had been witness to one of America's most enduring moments: the swearing-in of President Lyndon Johnson on the fateful flight from Dallas, Texas, with the body of former President John Kennedy in the cargo hold. The Secret Service controlled entrance to the plane itself and escorted visitors to the main cabin, where the Vice President and I were working. The door to the private office on Air Force Two opened and the agent in charge announced, "you have company."

My initial reaction to Truly was surprise. From his résumé I expected a more imposing figure, with more test pilot swagger and assertiveness. He is, in fact, a relatively soft spoken and somewhat hesitant or shy person. His gentle Southern accent and compact frame combined to create the impression of a friendly neighbor in a small southern town.

After introductions were made and pleasantries exchanged, the Vice President came to the point at hand: "The President would like to nominate you to be the NASA administrator. How do you feel about that?"

Truly smiled, paused, and replied, "I would be honored, Mr. Vice President."

"There's a lot of work that needs to be done at NASA. Are you sure you are up to the task?"

"I am, Mr. Vice President."

"I want to make sure that you will work with the National Space Council. We can do things in the White House that may be difficult for you to do from inside NASA, but we need your support."

"You have my word that we will make this work."

And then Truly left. Quayle picked up the phone and called Sununu to report he had met with Truly, he seemed like a good guy and he had no objection to forwarding the nomination to the Hill.

I wouldn't really have a chance to get to know Truly well for another month, until after he was confirmed by the Senate in May.

V.

"IF YOU DON'T KNOW WHERE YOU ARE GOING, ANY ROAD WILL TAKE YOU THERE."

Lewis Carroll

From the beginning of the new administration, there were calls for new initiatives and new goals for the civil space program. The National Academy specifically called a manned mission to Mars or lunar bases as possibilities, as well as a "Mission to Planet Earth", a new national mission aimed at earth observation. Others focused solely on the case for Mars over the advantages of lunar exploration alone. At the same time, many outside interest groups and NASA officials began to inquire as to the plans for the 20th anniversary of the lunar landing of Apollo XI. They asked if the White House wanted the lead on the event or whether NASA should take responsibility. I talked with Quayle and his Chief of Staff, Bob Guttman, about this and we all readily agreed that the White House and the Space Council should take the lead for whatever events took place. We let NASA know and I discussed with the Council staff how to engage on the topic.

It was obvious to me from the start that we could use the anniversary and the natural platform it would afford to do three things at once: reestablish the authority of the President to set the agenda for the civil space program and NASA; give NASA the top cover necessary to review, rationalize, and streamline its entire program plan, especially the Space Station Freedom; and finally, reignite America's flagging interest in our space program by setting a bold new national goal. Only later did it occur to me that, perhaps even more importantly, a new national space initiative might also provide a critical lifeline for an economically vital aerospace and advanced technology community that was facing a huge financial and workforce cliff as the Cold War began to thaw. In addition if done with significant Russian participation, this would give a critical financial and psychological boost to a collapsing Soviet Union and what would emerge as "the new Russia".

In early May I assembled the Space Council staff and explained that I was working on a concept that would require all our attention, and absolute discretion. I repeated the ground rules for emphasis and to make sure there was no doubt about my seriousness.

I said I was considering proposing to the President that he use the 20th anniversary of the Apollo moon landing to announce a new national space goal: a manned mission to the moon, or Mars, or both. For a moment there was silence, and then the questions started flying from the team. "Is it Mars, or is it Moon and Mars?" "How much will it cost?" "How long will it take?" "Do we do it alone or should we invite other nations to participate, as we've done with the Space Station Freedom program?" "What does it mean for the Space Station Freedom? What does it mean for the shuttle?" "Can NASA handle this? Is its plate already too full?"

"These are precisely the questions we have thirty days to answer," I replied, "And I remind you, if any of this leaks out, we will have not only created a major potential embarrassment for the President, we will be guilty of a cardinal sin of Presidential staff assistance: we would run the risk of forcing the President of the United States into a corner or preempting a decision he may not want to make."

We then started an intensive assessment of the parameters for a program of space exploration. We assessed the case for a return to the Moon and the case for a direct mission to Mars. We considered the pros and cons of international participation and whether that participation could be allowed on "the critical path", that is to say, whether successful completion of the enterprise would be dependant on the performance of one or more foreign entities. We tried to bound the costs and we looked at new technology.

The central problem with a direct mission to Mars is the incredible distance involved and the time delays in communication and transit. The Moon is a mere 250,000 miles from the Earth; the transit takes a couple of days and communications from the moon are delayed by only a second or two. Mars, on the other hand, is 25 million miles from Earth at its closest point; transit there would take over six months and communications would be delayed by almost an hour. Simple emergency planning and protocols for a mission to Mars must include matters of triage: there can be no Apollo XIII on a mission to Mars. Even baseline plans must include a provision that one or more astronauts would perish on the mission. This is the strongest case for a return to the Moon first. With two-day transits and no communication gaps, whole systems can be tested for space transit and for planetary habitation and survival. And there is still good science to be done on the Moon.

The question is then, do you take the high risk approach, with a somewhat reduced cost profile and faster potential achievement of the ultimate goal and go straight for Mars, or do you take the more conservative approach, relying on a more measured method of technology development and testing, sacrificing cost and schedule to the criteria of safety and incremental development and start with a return to the Moon? Although the advocates for both approaches were strong and sometimes emotional, in 1989 there simply was not a credible case to be made for a high-wire program of direct assault on Mars. We knew that if we were to convince the President, and then Congress, that America was ready for a new challenge in space exploration at all, a Manhattan- or Apollo-like crash program was simply not going to sell. After all, what would be the urgency? Why now? With whom would we be competing? Why take the high risk of failure or catastrophe? What justification could there be for so much risk and so much cost at this time?

Having decided to make a case inside the White House for the "Moon *and* Mars" proposal we assessed the general applicability of the existing human

spaceflight missions, the shuttle and Space Station Freedom, and then developed a reasonable plan for planetary exploration. We readily concluded the
obvious: neither the shuttle nor the Space Station was well adapted to efficient,
long term planetary exploration, and indeed, in the interim each would be
enormous resource competitors for the developments necessary to accomplish
either a Moon or Mars excursion efficiently. The shuttle was simply to fragile, too costly, and too limited, and the station was already burdened with
too many missions and functions to serve as an efficient node for in-orbit
assembly and as an operational base. The last thing we wanted to do was add
additional requirements to a Space Station design that was already strained
by weight, power, cost, and schedule. Additionally, the National Academy had
already observed in its recommendation to the President—elect that the Space
Station should be configured exclusively to provide the necessary life science
work to enable long-duration human space exploration. We naively reasoned
that NASA, once given a new exploration mission, would use the opportunity
to rationalize both the shuttle and the station in order to serve the new goal.

As to international cooperation, we all agreed that the simple imperatives
of cost and risk, and the precedent of the Space Station, meant that cooperation would be a necessary element of this new proposal. After all we made the
case that cooperation rather than competition would be an essential element
of space exploration, we could scarcely argue that for what would be the most
important mission since Apollo we would "go it alone".

Technology and program management were issues the entire Space Council
team easily agreed upon. We would encourage NASA to run this program with
the philosophy that was gaining credence in the Defense department, largely
through the demonstrated success of the SDI program: namely, "faster, cheaper,
and better". I had staffed the Space Council with several people from the
SDI program, including Air Force Colonel Pete Worden, who had managed
several of the space experiments that proved that you could achieve more, for
less, and in a shorter time than by utilizing a new approach to space acquisition. We envisioned a new space exploration initiative to be a complement to
SDI, even to the point of thinking about joint developments, as in the area of
space launch.

Finally we tackled the issue of cost. What would be a responsible and justifiable cost figure to bring to the President? We knew that conventional cost analysis, especially routine NASA cost analysis, would be high – really high. But we didn't want to be guilty of the same false claims that led NASA administrator James Beggs to tell President Reagan that the Space Station could be built in ten years for $8 billion. There had been some studies that put the cost of a mission to Mars in excess of $100 billion by utilizing many international "off the shelf" pieces, such as Russian heavy launch. We thought that using international cooperation to share costs could reduce the US burden, but would require yielding substantial work-share and critical path control. This was just too hard to work given the short time period we had and the secrecy we needed to preserve. Already some whom we queried about this or that fact or estimate or plan were beginning to connect the dots and sense that the White House might be working on a new initiative.

We settled on a total program cost estimate of $200 billion, with opportunities to save based on program management (faster, cheaper, better) and the degree of international work-share and responsibility and, most importantly, how aggressively NASA rationalized existing programs to meet the new mission. For a twenty-year program we reasoned that NASA would need to either free up or obtain new allocations for $10 billion a year. The shuttle and station together already cost almost $3 billion a year and were ramping up close to $6 billion at the peak, and so it seemed plausible that we could phase-out the station and shuttle and phase-in the new space exploration initiative without raising NASA's annual appropriation by more than 10% over time, from roughly $12 billion in FY89 to $13 billion in FY90. We were ready to start the internal coordination process.

VI.

A New Vision for a Post Cold War Exploration: This Time Together

It was late May and President Bush was consumed by preparations for the upcoming NATO summit in Brussels. It would be his first NATO summit and there was mounting pressure to clarify his national security vision beyond a continuation of that of the Reagan administration. Things were moving quickly, as he and Brent Scowcroft document in great detail in their outstanding and comprehensive work *A World Transformed*. Early on, the President assembled a "core group", as they were to call it, to exchange thoughts and ideas about redefining US relationships with Europe and the Soviet Union. Scowcroft recalls the pressure that Gorbachev was putting on the United States with his bold challenges and unilateral declarations. On the one hand, Scowcroft worried that US influence might be eroded in Europe if the Soviet leader was perceived as showing more aggressiveness and creativity than the US in advancing issues that directly affected European security and relief from defense spending. On the other hand, Scowcroft worried that too much aggressiveness on the part of the US, without bilateral agreements and concrete plans for action, could be a trap for the US, leading to unilateral concessions that could not be undone and affording the Soviets new advantages to exploit.

At one such "core group" meeting in the spring, Scowcroft recalls, "I introduced a version of an initiative I had first made to the President during the transition: the withdrawal of both US and Soviet ground forces in Central Europe… Dick Cheney looked stunned."[9] Later, as preparations for the May NATO summit began to finalize, Scowcroft and Cheney agreed on a plan to propose bilateral 25% reductions in central front forces and floated the proposal to the Chairman of the Joint Chiefs, Admiral William Crowe, at a meeting in Kennebunkport, Maine, a week before the summit began. According to Scowcroft, "Crowe reacted with alarm. He declared reductions of that dimension would force a drastic change in NATO strategy."[10]

The dim outlines of a likely "post Cold War defense posture" were emerging, and it clearly included major reductions in forces. That, matched with mounting pressure created by the size of the federal deficit, meant that a smooth "glide path" for defense would be a critical management challenge in the coming years. No one anticipated the speed and completeness of the collapse of the Soviet Union over the next eighteen months. And no one was prepared for the impact that collapse would have on the thinking and plans of the Department of Defense and the aerospace industry.

Although these discussions took place within a very small group in the White House, the fallout from this analysis was trickling down to the rest of the administration, including to the National Space Council staff. In early May, Condoleezza Rice of the National Security Council staff called and asked to meet with me on the topic of potential US-Soviet space cooperation. I had never met Condi before, but I knew of her through my close connections with Senator Pete Wilson's office and her recent posting at Stanford University. Condi is incredibly smart and a genuinely nice person. She is patient, earnest, and careful with her words. After a few minutes of small talk and connecting through people we knew in common, Condi asked about US-Soviet space cooperation. "Are there projects that we could pursue that would be beneficial to the United States?" What, she wanted to know, did I see as the potential payoffs in new space cooperation and what would be the risks?

I asked her what was motivating these questions and she replied that the administration was conducting an overall review of US-Soviet relations, and trade and scientific cooperation were topics under consideration. I asked her assessment of the status of the Soviet Union and she provided a detailed and serious analysis of the constitutional changes in Poland and what it meant for movements in Hungary, Czechoslovakia, and the northern states of Latvia, Lithuania, and Estonia. She said that, while it was clear that Gorbachev was preaching glasnost for Eastern Europe, it was not clear whether this was entirely a voluntary initiative. She was concerned that it might actually be an indicator of "troubles within" – of an empire stretched politically and economically too thin.

On May 31, I delivered a memorandum to Condi entitled "National Space Council Point Paper on US-Soviet Space Cooperation". In it, I observed that "a prudent long-term policy regarding cooperation with the Soviet Union in space should proceed from direct technical or economic benefit to the United States, distinct and separate from bilateral political considerations. It is important that the United States maintain a consistent international space cooperation policy and avoid dangerous tradeoffs between technical and political objectives." With these cautions in mind, I concluded that "joint US-Soviet space activities can provide net scientific, technical, or economic benefits to the United States if they are carefully conceived and managed."

We specifically identified four areas of potential cooperation that could conceivably pass these tests: joint long-term manned missions to Mars; joint short-term manned missions, such as a program to fly Soviet cosmonauts on the Space Shuttle and US astronauts on the MIR space station; joint space science missions, such as a joint Mars sample return mission; or, finally, cooperation on a specific space program, such as mitigating and limiting space debris.

Our net assessment of risk and reward led to a recommendation of either "arms length scientific cooperation in the context of broader international efforts", or "strictly limited short-term joint manned missions" focused on "obtaining access to Soviet medical data on the effects of long duration space-flight on humans[, as] this data has not been as well collected as it should be given the Soviet opportunities with MIR, due to poorly calibrated instruments and lack of Cosmonaut cooperation." We observed that "[t]his type of data could be very useful to future US space exploration if it could be obtained without a long-term manned commitment."

When I delivered the memorandum to Condi, I told her that we were very concerned about technology transfer, especially as it might relate to long-term autonomous space operations, an area of significant and important US advantage. We also worried about the general attitude in the scientific community that science knows no bounds and therefore significant space collaboration could be the source of important technology transfer. It is interesting to note that less than three years later, not long after the collapse of the Soviet Union, as our efforts at initiating long-term plans for human exploration were stalling (in no small measure because of the obstacles presented by the stubbornly non-responsive process of planning for Space Station Freedom), we initiated the Shuttle/MIR program precisely to gain the knowledge we needed on the effects long duration spaceflight has on humans – a problem that a "redesigned and streamlined" space station should have focused on.

It was against this backdrop that I began the process of testing the proposal we were recommending: that, on July 20, 1989, the President announce a plan for Americans to return to the Moon, and then proceed to Mars.

I went to see the Vice President. We met in his ceremonial office in the Old EOB. It is a spectacular room with high ornate ceilings, intricate inlaid tile flooring, and dramatic sea green walls covered with decorative trim that resembling stylized waves of gold. The room was renovated when George H. W. Bush had been Vice President, and it had initially served as the office of the Secretary of the Navy when it opened in 1888 – a time when the entire federal government was housed in the one building. Beneath the window overlooking the White House, there was a large credenza displaying behind glass large models of sailing ships and early warships. The story is often told of the Secretary of Navy, Joephus Daniels, whose desk in 1913 sat in the center of that room, and his young assistant Secretary of Navy whose eyes constantly drifted from the Secretary through the window to the White House. "Concentrate, Franklin," Daniels is alleged to have frequently admonished his young assistant. "There will be plenty of time later to consider occupancy of that building." And in due time, Franklin Roosevelt did.

The office had also been famously occupied by Franklin's distant cousin, Theodore, Assistant Secretary of the Navy in 1897. A portrait of TR was mounted near the Vice President's desk in order to serve, as Quayle told me, "as a constant reminder of 'the man who is in the arena'."

Quayle and I were always happy when I visited his office, and we normally took time to discuss a wide range of topics beyond the matters of my charge. Today, however, I got straight to the point.

"As you know," I began, "in just under ninety days it will be the twentieth anniversary of Apollo XI. I propose that we use that opportunity for President Bush to announce a new national space goal: a return to the Moon and then mounting an expedition to Mars."

To my surprise, Quayle didn't flinch. He said, "OK. Tell me more about it."

I told him about our quiet preliminary work and that we had concluded that the proposed mission include *both* destinations, the Moon and Mars, although there was a vocal constituency for a direct expedition to Mars. The Space Council staff, however, recommended both destinations, primarily based on concerns about risk and timing. We recommended further that, in consideration of affordability and recognized that without the national urgency that had driven the Apollo and Manhattan projects, the program could follow a long-term and measured approach. I said that we recommended a significant element of international cooperation in the program to continue. And I explained that we recommended the program be managed with the new ideas of faster, cheaper, better, and that it be heavily leveraged by rapid technology development and new ways of thinking and doing things.

"How much do you think it will cost and how long do you think it should take?"

I told the Vice President that it could be a twenty- or even thirty-year project that, in sum, would cost hundreds of billions of dollars, but that it could be managed year-to-year with only about a 10 to 15% increase in the NASA budget.

"Can NASA actually handle this?" he asked. "Is there any thought to establishing joint management with Defense or Energy, or even a new organization, like the SDIO?"

I was really taken aback by his questioning NASA's capability, and yet immediately understood its importance. My own initial assessment of NASA had included a relatively pessimistic view of its ability to manage and control large projects in terms of cost, schedule, and requirement management. And my thinking assumed that NASA would completely embrace the call for a new national mission in space and aggressively reprioritize and rationalize existing programs to accommodate and advance that new mission. I hadn't really thought about what would happen if they didn't.

"That's a very good question," I admitted, "and, no, I haven't discussed this with NASA leadership – security and confidentiality were our highest priorities."

Quayle said, "Let's discuss this with Sununu and Darman, and you talk to Truly. Perhaps I'll raise the issue with the President at lunch this week just to gauge his level of comfort. For now, though, let's consider this an interesting proposal, worthy of further consideration, but not yet ready to go to the President for his decision."

"What do *you* think?" I asked.

"Actually, I like it for a variety of reasons. I think, realistically, we are headed for a very uncertain future and lots of changes are possible. It is not inconceivable that our aerospace and defense industries could be in for very rough times, and we need their technology innovation and workforce development for our continued economic vitality. This initiative might just be a bridge to the future for them. NASA is clearly floundering and this could be an opportunity for internal reform and, frankly, a test of their capacity. Finally, we are looking for ways to keep America in an active leadership role in international relations after the Cold War, and large science endeavors that bring people together with common goals may be the kind of things we need for the world of tomorrow."

We had taken the first step.

I immediately called the NASA administrator's office to speak with newly-confirmed Dick Truly. I was told that he was in the air, returning to Washington from a visit to Houston, and would be in late. I was reminded that both he and I were scheduled to speak at a NASA-sponsored conference the next morning downtown and I could meet with him there.

I was scheduled to speak at the conference at 8:30 in the morning and Dick was to follow at 9:30. My topic was the new National Space Council. I would discuss our charter, our authority, and our vision for the US space program. Although I had developed some strong opinions about the state of various elements of the space program, I didn't want to conduct a program review in public, and so I planned to simply emphasize the organization and our charter and leave observations about the state of the overall program for a later time. I would, however, underscore that, in my opinion, "we generally need to do things faster, cheaper, and better in order to maintain our leadership in space."

At about 8:00am Dick Truly, his deputy, J.R. Thompson, and Frank Martin, head of the Office of Human Exploration, gathered in the small speaker's room just off the floor of the Omni Shoreham Hotel auditorium where the conference was getting under way. There were a couple of employees and staff assistants hovering around the coffee, juice, and doughnuts in the room and I politely, but firmly, asked everyone except Truly and J.R. to leave.

J.R. is a large man with a broad grin and a (seemingly permanent) pipe attached to his mouth. J.R. can summon himself to create a physically imposing appearance and his southern drawl was more sheriff than shop keep. I liked J.R., but over the next two and one-half years he proved to be NASA's most visible and aggressive defender – and the Space Council was frequently his target. At the Marshall Space Flight Center in Huntsville, Alabama – where he had been Center Director – he had earned the nickname "Rocket Bob". He had all the assuredness and cockiness that Truly lacked. They seemed a perfect fit. Only years later was I to learn that, in fact, Senator Howell Heflin (D-AL) had promoted Thompson for the top NASA job, in competition to Truly, and their partnership was more institutional than personal.

Truly was clearly made nervous by the circumstances of my urgent request to meet. He was *very* new in his capacity as administrator and didn't know what to expect.

I started much the same as I had with the Vice President.

"We are looking at the anniversary of Apollo XI to make an announcement of a new goal for the American space program," I said. I told him that we were recommending a call for a return to the Moon and then a manned mission to Mars.

Truly looked stricken.

"I don't think NASA can handle this right now", he said. "Our plate is already too full with the Space Station, the large observatory program, and the coming planetary missions. I just don't think we have the capacity. Let me think about it and get back to you tomorrow."

J.R. chimed in: "Do you think the Congress would fund this, with the Space Station just ramping up? Hell, we're looking at big cuts in the station already."

I told them that our hope and expectation was that NASA would take this new initiative as an opportunity to rationalize ongoing programs, to redirect ongoing efforts, and to streamline other initiatives so that this new vision would become the central organizing mission for the entire agency. I suggested that if we offered a compelling vision for the future of NASA and human spaceflight, Congress would work with them to create a new NASA.

They both nodded, but one look in their eyes made it clear that NASA was not going to uncritically embrace this idea.

It was early the next morning, about 7:30am, when I was told that Admiral Truly was on the phone.

"Hi Mark. I have given what you said yesterday lots of thought and I must admit you took me a bit by surprise with your idea. But hey, that doesn't matter. I wanted to let you know that, of course, NASA is ready to take on this challenge and we will make it work. I know that you haven't yet gotten agreement from the President on the plan, and that security is of the utmost importance, but I would like your agreement for me to bring a couple of people here at NASA into the project so that we will be prepared to answer questions when and if the President decides to do so."

I asked who he had in mind and Truly said, "I am thinking of Johnson Space Center director Aaron Cohen and Frank Martin, from here at headquarters."

I agreed, but cautioned Truly that I didn't want to see or hear anything about this coming from NASA sources and I asked him to make sure that NASA didn't start "anchoring" on any particular architecture or approach to the plan, as we had strong ideas about how the program should be structured and managed.

He paused and tentatively asked, "You're not thinking of anybody but NASA managing the program are you?"

I assured him that NASA would be right in the middle of whatever the President would decide. I don't think he was completely reassured.

With this important contact completed, I called the Vice President and reported on my meeting with Truly and his call the next day. "What?" said Quayle, "They actually turned you down at first? That's just incredible. Here we offer them the opportunity of a lifetime, and say we may be able to deliver the President of the United States no less, and they hesitate? I guess they *are* in trouble over there. I will set up a meeting with Darman and Sununu right away."

"Did you mention this to the President?" I asked.

"Briefly," he said, "He was concerned about the cost and how we would pay for it, but he was generally positive. I think we may have a shot."

It was later that day that Bob Grady, Darman's Program Area Director for science, energy, environment, and space, came to our office to find out what was up.

Grady is a fascinating and extremely talented man. He came to the Bush team from Governor Kean's administration in New Jersey, where he had been a policy advisor and speechwriter – a skill that was employed to great effect in the Bush-Quayle campaign. Bob is a tall, trim man with dark hair rapidly receding from the front of his broad head, and balanced by almost shoulder-length locks in the back. His Ivy League demeanor belied the fact that Grady came from rather humble beginnings in New Jersey. He was an amazing combination of elitism and street smarts. Like Darman, a Harvard graduate, Grady was incredibly hardworking and knowledgeable and was without a doubt Darman's most trusted assistant at OMB. These were two very smart men in a White House that had more than its share of brainpower.

Grady breezed into my office and said, "Alright, Albrecht, what are you up to? Trip to Mars perhaps?"

I smiled.

"Actually, this isn't such a bad idea," he went on, "We have taken a look at the cost of such an effort and it is expensive, but if we start slow and take a long view, I think we can make a case."

I walked Bob through our thinking, some of the work we had done, and why we concluded on the Moon *and* Mars, as well as on international cooperation, a long term vision, and the faster, cheaper, and better approach.

"You guys love SDI, don't you?" he asked. "Hey, don't get me wrong: I hope you are right. NASA has done a miserable job on the Space Station and they could use some new ideas."

I told Grady my view was that NASA could take this new initiative and use it for substantial reform of the organization and its program elements. In my opinion, simply laying this on top of the existing program would be a deadweight and non-starter.

He cautioned against being too aggressive and potentially jeopardizing the Station by undermining its value. "We could be left with nothing if we aren't careful," he warned.

The next day we met in the Vice President's West Wing office: the President's Chief of Staff Governor Sununu, Dick Darman, Bob Grady, and me.

Quayle started by saying that the Space Council staff had come up with a proposal for long-term human space exploration to the Moon and then on to Mars, and that we proposed that the President use the 20th anniversary of Apollo XI to announce it. He immediately explained that our concept was for a long-term goal, not a crash program, and that we would look to a broad technology program emphasizing new ideas and new approaches to space operations. He reported that NASA initially had a negative reaction to the idea, but came around — in his opinion as much from defensiveness as from fully embracing the concept.

Sununu responded that he thought going back to the Moon was boring, but acknowledged that a trip to Mars directly might be too big a leap without any compelling urgency to do so. He asked how this would fit into ongoing programs, particularly the Space Station, and he asked Darman how much it would cost.

Darman reached out his hand to Grady, who opened a large file and handed a specific page from it to Darman. Darman proudly surveyed the page and said, "We have already looked at this and we think that total program cost would be in the range of $200 to $300 billion dollars."

"How long should we provide?" asked Sununu.

"At least twenty years," said Darman, "maybe longer. After all, we said this is not to be a crash program."

"If we make it thirty," said Sununu, "then we are talking about putting a man on Mars before the 50th anniversary of Apollo XI."

Darman said, "If we start gradually and then phase the program in, we can make this work with only about a 10% increase in spending."

"Perfect," said Quayle, "I'll discuss this with the President: a return to the Moon and then exploration of Mars, with a goal of humans on Mars before the 50th anniversary of Apollo XI."

"There is one more item." I interjected. "NASA. Do we think that NASA, as it is currently constituted, is up to this task? After all, their initial reaction to the idea was that their plate was too full with the Station, Mission to Planet Earth, and the upcoming interplanetary probes. They didn't think they had the capacity to take on this new goal."

"If they are not," shot back Sununu, "then we will get rid of them. Seriously, this is a test for the agency. I went to graduate school working on a NASA grant, but I wouldn't blink an eye at shutting them down if they proved too stale and unimaginative to implement this plan."

"We have to be careful," said Darman, "The support for space is fragile and if we become too aggressive we could risk the whole program and be left with nothing."

"But we can't afford to do both," said Quayle. "We have to make sure NASA gets with the program."

Cynthia appeared at the door, "Governor, the President is asking for you in the Oval."

The meeting quickly adjourned. Darman and Grady agreed to work up a specific budget proposal for the initiative and we agreed to start low-level coordination on the announcement. Two days later I got a call from the Vice President.

"The President has approved in concept the program and the announcement. Let's start preparations for a major announcement in July."

VII.

THE PROOF

"Faced with the choice between changing one's mind and proving that there is no need to do so, almost everyone gets busy on the proof."
John Kenneth Galbraith

As the spring of 1989 wore on, it became increasingly clear that the federal deficit was a serious and urgent problem and was beginning to dominate the entire budget process. As the markups from the authorizing and then appropriating committees began to work their way from committee to floor to conference, we found ourselves dealing with more and more spending issues. The National Aerospace Plane (NASP) which was initiated in the Reagan administration as a joint NASA and DoD development – designed as a hypersonic airplane capable of traveling from Los Angeles to Tokyo in under three hours, to be developed ultimately into a single-stage-to-orbit, fully recoverable space vehicle – was in serious trouble on the Hill and within the two departments. The Space Council urgently met in late June to shore up NASP's support within the government and in Congress, where it was facing severe cuts and financial fratricide between DoD and NASA. The Space Station Freedom was also under intense budget pressure, and cuts in the FY90 budget were signaling real difficulties in the out years, when the program was to ramp up significantly.

On the house side, the NASP had been cut in the NASA appropriations to $33 million, down from a budget request of $127 million, and the Space Station had been cut $395 million, from a request of $690 million. The defense appropriators had shown a similar degree of constraint in spending, especially for new initiatives like the NASP and other space-related programs, such as new launch capabilities. Already the term "peace dividend" was working its way into the congressional lexicon and appropriators' mindsets. The DoD space launch fleet – resurrected only a year before the Challenger accident, primarily at the insistence and force of personal efforts by Air Force Secretary Pete Aldridge – a so called "complementary expendable launch vehicle program" (CELV), was composed of early ICBM vintage launch vehicles gradually and unsystematically upgraded for additional performance, was saved from cancellation at the last moment. Not surprisingly, these converted ICBMs had become costly and cumbersome to operate. The evolved behemoth Titan IV launcher, capable of launching the largest payloads comparable to a full "shuttle load", was literally built on the launch pad and took over eighteen months to prepare for launch.

It was becoming painfully obvious that we were presiding over the slow demise of many Reagan era space initiatives and a civil and defense space infrastructure that was suffering inattention. At the same time we were looking at what could arguably be considered the biggest space initiative since Apollo.

We were facing a crucial point in the space enterprise and *our* conclusion was that in order for it to survive, it had to be shaken up. The risk, as clearly identified by Dick Darman in the White House and Dick Truly and the NASA team, was that if we miscalculated on the appeal of a major overhaul, if we upset the delicate but inefficient interest network that supported the current NASA program, we ran a significant risk of losing it all. What a terrible choice: durable mediocrity, stagnation, and waste, or a zero-sum, win-or-lose-it-all gamble with an aggressive restart to human spaceflight. I pointed this out to the Vice President: "We are looking at a high risk approach."

He didn't blink and said, "Let's not settle for mediocrity."

On June 15, I met in my White House office with the NASA team charged with providing a first-blush concept for meeting the new exploration goals. The team was composed of both old NASA hands – like Aaron Cohen, director of the Johnson Space Center, a genial engineer short on political sophistication and fiercely loyal to NASA as an institution – as well as enthusiastic young turks – like Mark Craig, a strawberry blond house of a man with an eager and sunny disposition who looked like a starting guard on the Dallas Cow-boys. I sensed in the NASA team some of the conflicting strategies we were experiencing with OMB in the White House. Cohen had his marching orders: Space Shuttle as the transportation baseline, Space Station completion *as-is* first, Space Station as the transfer node for lunar and then Martian explora-tion next. These ground rules were non-negotiable. Craig seemed more flexible when questioned about the use of alternative architectures and technologies for achieving the long-term goals more efficiently, without regard to current program designs; but Cohen clung to the "ah shucks, I'm not sure what exactly you are looking for" approach. He smiled and nodded and kept returning to the refrain, "I'm not really sure what you mean by 'new technologies and archi-tectures'." Never challenging, never questioning the reasoning, simply looking perplexed in a pleasant sort of way. The NASA formulation of alternatives, of course, not only completely preserved the current baseline, it also isolated the new initiative, hanging it outside and exposed in the program plan. It was a statement simply inferred – an add-on to the existing program, completely separate and outside the baseline. And then came the price tag: $400 billion dollars.

(A note to the reader: At the end of the nineteenth century, when many growing cities in the United States were still working on basic infrastructure, sandbags were frequently used as makeshift retaining walls and conduits for all manner of civil engineering maintenance projects. By the 1880s these ubiq-uitous and handy public building blocks became the favorite weapon of bullies and petty criminals, who used them to bludgeon unsuspecting passersby before robbery; the practice became known as "sandbagging" and quickly thereafter came to refer to anything that would lull or stun someone into a false sense of either the strength or weakness of another, only to be "robbed" in the end by surprise.)

In 1986, NASA Administrator Jim Beggs may have retired the "sandbag-ging cup" when he oversold and under estimated the cost of the Space Station to President Reagan by a country mile, or several country miles – but this NASA team had to be a close second, as it had gold plated and "risked down" this initiative to the point where it would stagger the entire federal budget for decades. In the case of the Station, the sandbagging was to entice the President to commit to the project; in the case of the exploration initiative, it appeared as though it was to cripple the new initiative in favor of preserving the baseline. We did not have time to sort out cost estimating before the intended announcement date of July 20, but "the NASA plan" did do enough damage to force us to water down the President's announcement with regard to specific dates and the outlines of the program plan in order to avoid appearing to embrace the NASA baseline. And it caused us to recognize that NASA may well not partner with us on the vision of the plan. When eventually announced on July 20, the President charged "the Vice President and the Space Council to come up with a plan for achieving these goals". This was neither a casual nor incidental matter.

VIII.

WHERE WOULD WE BE TODAY IF PRESIDENT KENNEDY HAD "TESTED" REACTION TO HIS RICE SPEECH?

After the initial briefings from NASA and our subsequent agreement based on their "baseline plan" that we would focus on a long-term vision for lunar and Martian exploration rather than on the first blush program details, we began a round of presentations at the White House in order to start consensus-building toward support of an announcement on July 20 of a Presidential goal for human space exploration.

During the week of July 3, we invited core space supporters, members of the space science community, aerospace executives, and congressional staff down to the White House to talk about next steps in space exploration and a vision for long-term human spaceflight. While we were able to establish predictable support from the primary interest groups of space enthusiasts, those right in the middle of the budgetary squeeze, the contractors and congressional staffers, were more skeptical — after all, they had the most invested in the status quo and the most to lose by any change. They were already hunkering down in the face of stiff fiscal restraint to preserve as much of their own programs as they possibly could. Radical change, however appealing to their sense of progress, was overtaken by concerns about preserving the status quo. The House majority clerk of the appropriations committee, Dick Malow, perhaps said it best when he reported years later that his "initial reaction was that maybe this is something that we ought to be doing, but I don't think I jumped in and said, 'That's the greatest idea in the world.' And as I started to see the details of it, as they unfolded, I became concerned, especially given the budget situation."[11]

The CEOs of leading aerospace companies were invited to the White House on the afternoon of July 5. Not surprisingly, we had nearly 100% attendance, despite the fact that the day before had been the 4th of July holiday. Dan Tellep, the courtly and soft-spoken head of Burbank-based Lockheed, was there, as was Don Beall, the leader of Rockwell from Downey, California. Don is an interesting mix of accountant and cowboy, probably the most hard-boiled businessman of the bunch. His predecessor at Rockwell, Bob Anderson, was there as well; he was of the first generation of American aerospace leaders — a tough, hard-charging, hard-living, and risk-taking engineer that helped build a company and an industry from the ground and who knew each of his competitors personally. There was John McDonnell, son of Sandy McDonnell, founder of McDonnell aircraft in St. Louis. John looked every bit the part of a friendly Midwest middle manager, with a balding pate and tightly groomed beard. The professorial and brainy duo of Allen Puckett and Mal Currie of Hughes, recently acquired by GM, from El Segundo, California, were there, with probably no fewer than five PhDs between the two of them. Joe Gorman of TRW and Don Peterson of Ford were perhaps the oddest of the bunch. Peterson, who managed Ford Aerospace, was more of a car man than an aerospace executive, and Joe Gorman's classified space business was dominated by an auto-parts enterprise that always seemed to embarrass him. Stan Pace from General Dynamics, also in St. Louis, had just taken over from the legendary Dave Lewis and was in the process of cleaning up a series of serious ethical lapses inside the company that resulted in the dismissal of almost thirty executives and the retirement of Lewis himself. Tall and well dressed, Stan was clearly the smoothest operator in the room.

We started the presentation with my overview of the National Academy report and other advisory commentary, and explained that our space programs, both defense and especially civil, were under stress financially. I observed that the Cold War was showing signs of a thaw that would put into doubt long-term defense spending and that NASA's lack of a long-term vision was slowly eroding support for the core program. I repeated the National Academy's concerns about the NASA organization stemming from this lack of focus and said that President Bush was concerned about this situation but he remained committed to a strong and purposeful aerospace industry both for our national security and our technological and economic vitality. I explained that we were considering recommending that the President set a long-term goal for human space exploration that could unify NASA and its programs and avail itself of capacity that could be freed up from declining defense work. Dick Truly and his team then followed with a presentation of some technology and infrastructure ideas that might support a lunar base and Mars exploration. He was careful not to be too specific about details, but showed how, for example, the shuttle/station construct could support such an implementation. The Vice President joined us when we finished and he amplified the administration's concerns and commitment to the enterprise and then opened the floor to discussion.

There was polite interest, but, frankly, only a subdued reaction from the group, which came as a surprise to me and clearly to the Vice President as well. Why would those who stood to benefit the most from such a potentially enormous government program be so cautious and quiet?

Bob Anderson spoke first and expressed concerns about congressional support for such an effort and wondered where the money would come from. He said, "Frankly, we all love this idea, but times are extremely tough. Is this realistic?"

Quayle pointed out that creating an inspirational new initiative could revive interest in America's space program, lead the world in new, cooperative, as opposed to competitive, technology ventures, and buffer reductions in our defense programs with sustaining work on new aerospace technology. This generated some discussion about defense priorities and the need to avoid precipitous, imprudent, and risky "peace dividend" downsizing. The group slowly warmed, and by the end, when each was invited to comment, all were supportive of the idea, but cautioned against overreaching and overextending and thereby undermining momentum for existing programs.

Interestingly, within a day, several of these individuals either contacted me in person or by phone to privately elaborate. Anderson, McDonnell, Puckett, and Pace all contacted me. The calls were virtually identical. They said that while as Americans they were obviously encouraged by what clearly appeared to be a thawing of the Cold War, as leaders of America's technology infrastructure, they were deeply concerned by the current environment on the Hill, an environment that they feared was getting ahead of the facts on the ground. They specifically expressed concerns for both the civil and national security space programs. McDonnell said that his first priority to shareholders was to secure the current business base and defend it against draconian cuts. In the specific case of NASA, he said that McDonnell-Douglas was completely invested in one way or another in the existing shuttle and station programs. With his customer, Dick Truly, standing right in front of him, he could scarcely dissent from supporting the baseline program, and the indication they were already getting from their NASA customers was that any new initiatives would be treated strictly as "additive to the established baseline program, and not a substitute or replacement". Puckett and Pace completely agreed that NASA needed focus and that the potential of layoffs from defense downsizing on the horizon was causing serious internal reassessments within their companies. They too worried that NASA would be resistant to any change in the baseline program and therefore worried that a new initiative wouldn't be able to garner support. Bob Anderson was the most vociferous supporter of NASA and the existing program but concurred that "a new direction is probably needed." We had begun to see the undercurrents and potential impacts of a serious post-Cold War downsizing and the confused and near panic state in which it left aerospace leadership as it contemplated a sudden outbreak of peace.

One week later, columnists Rowland Evans and Robert Novak of the *Washington Post*, published a piece entitled, "Quayle's Ambitious Space Program." In it they reported:

Long distance planning by an administration better known for reacting rather than initiating might look like a moonbeam except for two truths; first, space to Bush and Quayle is a major foreign policy and technological challenge; second, Budget Director Richard Darman is a bona fide space junkie with a vision too spacious and vigorous to be confined by dollars and cents. As for the barons of the aerospace industry who were briefed on the Quayle proposals, they raised many hard questions but were generally favorable to the full program. One obvious reason for that is the probability that defense-space research, engineering, and production will begin to be phased out soon if Mikhail Gorbachev sticks with his peace campaign. If defense procurement funds are indeed made to shrivel, the first sacrifice will be research, development, and engineering money. That could fragment high-tech teams of space-age scientists and engineers working on military programs, splitting them up and endangering the nation's future security. If Bush buys Quayle's 20-year package, this priceless resource would find a second home.[12]

As I was later to discover, this same line of reasoning applied to our Soviet colleagues with even greater force, and, unbeknownst to me or anyone else in the administration at the time, it was significantly influencing Russian plans for post-Cold War "engagement" with the United States. In short, Russian academicians, politicians and industry managers had come to the same conclusions about life after the Cold War and were crafting their own plans to work together to keep their aerospace industry alive.

IX.

"LEAD, FOLLOW, OR GET OUT OF THE WAY."

Thomas Paine

It was a typical hot and humid July in Washington and the 20th was no exception. As the assembled crowd of several hundred sat patiently, if not comfortably, in the sun on the steps of the National Air and Space Museum, President Bush, Vice President Quayle, and the Apollo XI astronauts could clearly be seen inside the museum through the enormous glass windows that composed the Mall-side walls of the building. They were posing for photographs and admiring the artifacts along the interior promenade of the National Mall. Frankly, it was hot as hell and to the relief of all the party soon emerged and the President, flanked by the Apollo XI crew, stood on the steps of the National Air and Space Museum and spoke:

"In 1961 it took a crisis – the space race – to speed things up. Today we don't have a crisis; we have an opportunity. To seize this opportunity, I'm not proposing a 10-year plan like Apollo; I'm proposing a long-range, continuing commitment. First, for the coming decade, for the 1990s: Space Station Freedom, our critical next step in all our space endeavors. And next, for the new century: back to the Moon; back to the future. And this time, back to stay. And then a journey into tomorrow, a journey to another planet: a manned mission to Mars.

"Each mission should and will lay the groundwork for the next. And the pathway to the stars begins, as it did 20 years ago, with you – the American people. And it continues just up the street there, to the United States Congress, where the future of the Space Station and our future as a space-faring nation will be decided.

"And, yes, we're at a crossroads. Hard decisions must be made now as we prepare to enter the next century. As William Jennings Bryan said, just before the last turn of the century: 'Destiny is not a matter of chance; it is a matter of choice. It is not a thing to be waited for; it is a thing to be achieved.'

"And to those who may shirk from the challenges ahead, or who doubt our chances of success, let me say this: To this day, the only footprints on the Moon are American footprints. The only flag on the Moon is an American flag. And the know-how that accomplished these feats is American know-how. What Americans dream, Americans can do. And 10 years from now, on the 30th anniversary of this extraordinary and astonishing flight, the way to honor the Apollo astronauts is not by calling them back to Washington for another round of tributes. It is to have Space Station Freedom up there, operational, and underway, a new bridge between the worlds and an investment in the growth, prosperity, and technological superiority of our nation. And the Space Station will also serve as a stepping stone to the most important planet in the solar system: planet Earth.

"The Space Station is a first and necessary step for sustained manned exploration, one that we're pleased has been endorsed by Senator Glenn, and Neil Armstrong, and so many of the veteran astronauts we honor today. But it's only a first step. And today I'm asking my right-hand man, our able Vice President, Dan Quayle, to lead the National Space Council in determining specifically what's needed for the next round of exploration: the necessary money, man-power, and materials; the feasibility of international cooperation; and develop realistic timetables – milestones – along the way. The Space Council will report back to me as soon as possible with concrete recommendations to chart a new and continuing course to the Moon and Mars and beyond."

Later that afternoon, President and Mrs. Bush hosted a barbeque on the broad sloping south lawn of the White House, famous for the annual "Easter Egg Roll." The south lawn is also familiar as the scene of many historic departures: the launch pad for Marine One, the helicopter that transports the President to and from Andrews Air Force Base and Camp David. That day there was a large crowd of several hundred guests, dignitaries, and members of Congress with their families. There was old fashioned barbeque and country music, which gave the entire event the feel of a county fair. Naturally, the Apollo crew was the star of the show, constantly surrounded by admirers seeking photographs, autographs, and the chance to simply come near and touch "the men from the moon".

Getting the three of these men together in one place had been something of a feat. It had been many years since the three of these heroes had been together. In fact, as Buzz Aldrin confided to me that day, he hadn't seen Neil in over ten years. While Buzz and Michael Collins were fairly public people (though Michael notably less so than Buzz), Neil Armstrong had become something of a recluse post-Apollo. He retreated to his farm and business in Ohio soon after he left NASA and was rarely seen at public events, especially those that focused on Apollo or the space program, and never with his crewmates. He rejected numerous advertising and commercial opportunities, clearly preferring his privacy. We contacted him several weeks earlier about the anniversary and the White House event and he initially declined participation, telling me that he didn't feel comfortable with all the attention and rehashing of events from decades past. When I confided in him that the President was going to be doing more than simply commemorating Apollo XI, that he was, in fact, going to be setting a new course for exploration and that we needed the Apollo XI crew to help set that course, he agreed. But he did so reluctantly.

Neil Armstrong, tall and solid, a handsome but rather anonymous-looking man, has the quiet and calm demeanor of the middle American he clearly is. He was polite and thoughtful that day, but oddly distant — not in an arrogant manner, but rather with an "elsewhere" focus. I suppose he was exactly the same "steady stick" required those many years ago when he calmly forward-thrusted the Eagle past the intended landing site, over unforeseen lunar obstacles, with absolutely no clue as to what was available over the next rise, and with barely five seconds of propellant left, then dropped the craft gently to the little patch of the Moon that became "Tranquility Base".

Buzz Aldrin, on the other hand, is a bundle of energy in a compact package. He had a million ideas about the new exploration initiative and was extremely excited about all of them that day. The two astronauts are completely different personalities and not particularly close. One can only imagine the interaction as they waited almost eight hours on the surface of the Moon before disembarking onto its surface...and into history.

Michael Collins is the most "regular" of the three, is of medium build and height and very trim — almost thin — with a broad forehead. He is earnest but serious and mostly enjoys "real work and serious thinking". He had become a successful businessman in Texas, served on several corporate boards, and kept a low personal profile. One couldn't help but sympathize for the critical but clearly "supporting role" he had played in what can only be described as the greatest shared human drama of the modern age.

Standing in the crowd of people that day, hot and humid, looking back at the White House, the Truman porch, the grand spiral helix staircase to the West Room of the second floor, watching the President of the United States mingle among the crowd, talking about what he had said that day, talking with the Vice President of the United States while standing next to Neil Armstrong, Buzz Aldrin and Michael Collins, I couldn't help but think about where I was when these men stepped on to the surface of the moon.   How very far away that sunny day in La Jolla, California seemed to me now, and how incredibly improbable being here and in this circumstance would have seemed to me then.

As the day turned to evening and the White House staff slowly began to usher the celebrants from the south lawn to the gates on the east side of the White House, we retreated to our offices to talk with reporters to help shape their perceptions of the events of the day. The initial reactions to the President's remarks were predictable: there was no timetable; there was no program plan; we were in the midst of a budget crisis and this new national goal without details or a further explanation was viewed politely but necessarily skeptically. We were under no illusions that this speech alone would create a public groundswell and immediate congressional action on the initiative. We pointed to the history of the Kennedy speech at Texas A&M back in October 1961, when, in the reporting on the speech the next day, there had been scarcely a mention of the challenge to "put a man on the Moon within the decade". We had made compromises consciously and argued that this was the beginning of a long process, not an end in itself.

Four days later the Vice President wrote to Dick Truly, specifically requesting that "NASA provide a technical mission description which can serve as a baseline for review.... The baseline should be comprehensive and provide a zero-based assessment for Space Council consideration." He asked that NASA provide "an assessment of the technology required to support the program plan [and that] promising new technologies which offer substantial cost or schedule saving should be identified." He asked that NASA assess "the applicability of the current Space Station design and the feasibility of optimizing it to better support the new manned exploration objectives." And he asked that NASA evaluate "foreign participants [that] can make unique technical contributions or substantially reduce the cost of the program to the United States." And he asked that NASA report back to the Council in ninety days.

At the same time, I advised the Vice President that we would need to add to NASA's plan and develop a broader base of agency participation than NASA alone could provide. The Council staff recommended establishing a small group of outside citizens, a Blue Ribbon panel that could provide a sounding board for the Vice President as well as technical advice. And we recommend that the Vice President send a letter to the members of the Space Council outlining how we were to address this task. At his direction, I sent a memorandum to the members of the Space Council, outlining exactly these instructions, including a specific call to provide whatever assistance NASA requested in forming the baseline program plan. Despite our disappointment with NASA's unimaginative, costly, and conservative first response to the initiative, and its clear reluctance to open up its core programs to review in light of the new direction the President had provided, we were hopeful that our feedback and clear direction from the Vice President would guide NASA to look at alternative approaches to achieving the goal. We encouraged them to use advanced technologies, international capabilities (such as including Russian heavy lift launch resources), and restructured core programs, like the Space Station, to offer a rich menu of choices for the Council and the President in order to achieve the goals set that day.

It was hard to believe that in what seemed like the blink of an eye – scarcely four months into the Bush administration we were standing on the brink of the end of the Cold War, our nation's arsenal of freedom was at a crossroads, the nation's space program was teetering under its own weight, and the enormous Soviet military-industrial machine — largely concealed from us — was restive, starved, and unsettled, beginning to contemplate its place in a world of "demand" rather than "command" economics once it became freed from the heavy, however steady, hand of politburos and central committees and subjected to the largely unknown mercies of markets and money.

We had made our choices: to shake up the space program in order to revive it, to enlist the great engines of American technological achievement, to pivot and not pause in a new era of space exploration, and to create a new vision of American leadership through cooperation rather than competition in what would emerge as the post-Cold War world.

PART II

I.

THE SLOW REVEAL

It had been four months since the President's announcement, in July 1989, of plans for an American return to the Moon, this time to stay, and then a manned mission to Mars. NASA was working on a 90-day study on proposed architectures to accomplish the President's goal. The National Space Council was preparing the rest of the administration for the next phase of the initiative: a specific plan, with hard targets and dates, and detailed architectures to scrutinize, debate, and ultimately propose for congressional funding.

The Vice President's original charge to NASA – to provide the administration with alternative architectures based on different technologies, levels of risk, and general approaches to the exploration challenge – had been a point of contention with the Agency from the outset. Time and again, meeting after meeting, we pushed and prodded Dick Truly, Aaron Cohen, and Mark Craig to ensure that the final NASA product would not be a "point solution", that is, an up or down choice, but rather a menu of alternative paths with alternative technologies, alternative costs and risks, and alternative impacts on existing NASA plans. We insisted that this new initiative not be considered an add-on to the baseline NASA plan, but rather an organizing core for the entire agency agenda. We were determined to offer the President real choices and to offer NASA real opportunities to reorient the entire agency. During this time, as we prepared the community for what we envisioned as a high technology initiative with many new developments and innovations, our rhetorical description of the program with the National Academy of Sciences, with the committees on the

Hill, with the trade media, and with industry was increasingly diverging from what the 90-day study was actually preparing. NASA kept the work of the study group private, but we had enough contacts within the system to receive vague, but unambiguous signals about the direction of the work...and the signals were disappointing. We tried to remain optimistic, but as time wore on, it became increasingly obvious that NASA was on a path to do this their way.

On October 26, we convened a Space Council meeting to review the status of the President's exploration initiative. As the Vice President explained at the meeting, "Our job is to consider the policy building blocks for the initiative, identify critical issues that require executive level guidance, and above all make sure that the President has real, robust alternatives so that he can make informed decisions that will start the exploration initiative down the right path." Specifically, he emphasized that we "must explore program options, identify enabling technologies and consider the institutional issues associated with maintaining focus, momentum, and excellence over a sustained period." We would need to articulate the clear goals and objectives we sought through the involvement of international partners, including the Soviet Union. We emphasized that we would look to all departments and agencies to assist in technology identification and development as necessary, and expected all to act together to achieve the President's goals. It was clear to all that NASA's ongoing work on reference cases was specifically not to be considered as a baseline. The meeting was going smoothly and without controversy when, toward the end, OMB Director Dick Darman interjected. He said that, though we all were completely supportive of the President's space exploration initiative, reports coming to OMB from inside NASA indicated that NASA's study was, in fact, a baseline plan with only schedule excursions – exactly the opposite of what we had just agreed on. He said that cost, program, and schedule estimates contained in the draft 90-day report to the Council were in the range of one-half trillion dollars over a thirty-year period, starting with over a billion dollars in new funding immediately. And the working plans called for almost no new technology. The entire effort was simply added on top of NASA's existing baseline program. Darman claimed that this amounted to NASA recommending a program to the President that was not executable.

He said, "We don't want to put the President in the posture of appearing to slow down the initiative before it has even started. OMB has been urging NASA to develop a phased architectural approach to the initiative that focuses early work on highly leveraged technologies that could dramatically alter the total cost and schedule of the effort."

Truly was stunned. He clearly had no idea this issue would come up. He mumbled something about "informal staff working papers" and then gathered himself enough to reply that he would only provide responsible alternatives to the Council and the President. He then cautioned about "studying the problem to death" and Darman quickly responded that an approach that emphasized technology early with chances for breakthroughs in cost, performance, and schedule would actually be very robust and aggressive – hardly a "study it to death" approach. The matter ended with Admiral Truly promising to get personally involved in the work of the study group to make certain that anything brought forward was sound and achievable.

As the members of the Council and their staffs left the ornate Cordell Hull Conference Room in the OEOB that day, it was clear that NASA was isolating itself on the matter. The fact was that other departments and agencies had growing interests and potential equities in the new exploration initiative. NASA, in effect, was opening the door for other federal departments and agencies who were already contemplating new post cold war missions to step in and lay claim to a part of the program. The fact that Dick Darman was the "challenger" should have been an unmistakable warning to change course...it went unheeded.

II.

"LET ONE HUNDRED FLOWERS BLOSSOM."

Mao Zedong

The evolving situation in the eastern bloc of the Soviet Union that fall was not lost on those in the US national security community, both inside and outside the government. In fact, the day before the German announcement of free passage from east to west, Gerry Johnston, president of the McDonnell Douglas Corporation, visited me to discuss meetings he had just had in the Pentagon with members of the Joint Chiefs of Staff.

Gerry was a serious man and a veteran of decades in the aerospace industry. His demeanor that day was sober and concerned. It is customary in the fall for the Joint Chiefs to meet with the leaders of the aerospace community to discuss the upcoming DoD budget preparation process. The Chiefs have an important role to play in the annual Defense Department Program, Planning, and Budgeting System (PPBS) cycle by representing the operational commands at the resource table. They meet with industry leaders each year to discuss ongoing and planned activities as well as needs and deficiencies, and to share their thinking about requirements for the future. These conversations are important opportunities to set expectations and to help synchronize the industry with its customer. They are valued for their candor and frankness and are generally considered "private communications". Gerry had just finished his meetings and reported that the JCS had informed him that the forecast for the next ten years showed the United States reducing its core defense structure by at least one-third. Gerry said that, as he looked at the backlog and new business opportunities for McDonnell Douglas, he saw a dramatic change in the ten-year outlook from a largely defense dominated business plan to one where space would become the largest single business area. And McDonnell Douglas would become a much smaller company. He was very concerned about NASA and its future plans.

He also heard that NASA's response to the President's new exploration initiative was likely to be conservative, costly, and an "add on" to the baseline NASA program without deviation. Gerry said that he feared that such a plan, in the current budget environment and with anticipated cuts in defense spending as a result of the "peace dividend", would be a non-starter. He urged us to do everything in our power to persuade NASA to fully embrace the new opportunity and to make adjustments to the core program so as to persuade Congress that additional funding to the civil space program was efficient. He said that this project might well be the salvation of an aerospace industry facing brutal downsizing. Without acknowledging Gerry's premise, I told him that this had been an integral element of the President's thinking about the initiative from the start and that we, in turn, would need industry's support in order to reenergize the civil space enterprise with new and exciting goals and technology developments.

As the days passed and the Space Council meeting to review NASA's 90-day study approached, I received a call from Edward Teller at Lawrence Livermore's labs. Teller, the father of the hydrogen bomb, the innovation that took nuclear weapons from kilotons of power to megatons of power and, in his view, took nuclear conflict from only somewhat unthinkable by a reckless and megalomaniac Soviet Union to utterly unthinkable – making the hydrogen bomb the cornerstone of long-term, stable deterrence. I had first met Teller several years earlier, when I was working in the Senate on the SDI program. At that time he was already in his late seventies, with serious vision problems, an unsteady gait, and stooped posture that he compensated for with the aid of a long wooden staff making him look a like Moses as he ambled down the hallways of Congress.

Teller was a brilliant and complex man of vision and action who did not suffer fools gladly... and he was more than willing to identify the fools. He was at times quite charming, and his clipped Hungarian accent, exaggerated guttural rolls, and loud voice always commanded attention and respect, even if sometimes only grudgingly. He was a character, no doubt. We affectionately referred to him as "ET", intentionally invoking not only his monogram but his "other worldly" qualities as well.

In his characteristic manner Teller got right to the point: "Look, is the President really serious about space exploration? If he is, you *must* know that NASA is utterly incapable of doing anything useful – just look at the Space Station. We have heard what you and the Vice President have been saying about wanting to bring new approaches, new technologies, and new perspectives to the problem of human space flight, and my colleague Lowell Wood and a team at Livermore have a plan that does just that. It will take a fraction of the cost and time of any NASA plan and will reenergize space technology, create new industries, and pull along others internationally. But we won't deliver this plan to you for use as you see fit if you don't want it."

I asked about the Department of Energy and whether such a report, if made public, would cause them internal problems. Teller said, "Look, the DoE is completely aware of Lowell's work and recognizes the Lab's ability to pursue 'self directed' projects. We won't be causing any problems with them." I told him that I would have to think about it, but that we would get back to them very soon. I explained that we were thinking of convening a Blue Ribbon panel of experts to review the NASA 90-day study and that we would be honored to have him participate if he would be willing. Without hesitation he said, "Of course I would."

I was aware of the Livermore work as many members of the Space Council staff had long associations with Lowell Wood from the Strategic Defense Initiative, during which, Lowell had spearheaded work on the concept of Brilliant Pebbles, a cluster of small interceptors dispensed in space to engage nuclear warheads and decoys when launched by ballistic missiles. The concept was an elaboration on the early thought of "smart rocks" that could track and maneuver and run into warheads at astonishing rates of speed high while the warheads were in their ballistic trajectory; it was specifically designed to counter arguments that cheap and plentiful decoys could overwhelm such a defense. Lowell was also controversial. Even though he had enjoyed many successes, he had his notable failures as well. For example, his proposal to build a large X-ray laser in space that could lethally attack thousands of in-flight nuclear warheads with a single burst of x-rays funneled through multiple laser focal planes had been a dud. The reason was that the source of the incredible pulse of X-rays was to be a nuclear detonation. Thus, in order to blunt a nuclear attack, a space based nuclear detonation would be necessary. Killing nukes with nukes had never been a popular idea and the concept of testing such a device was unthinkable. Nevertheless, Lowell and the Livermore team needed to be taken seriously.

The basic thrust of the Livermore team's approach to space exploration was speed, safety, and simplicity. The presentation they had made to NASA in October was entitled, "An American-Traditional Space Exploration Program: Quick, Inexpensive, Daring, and Tenacious". At the core of the Livermore concept was the idea of "inflatable modules" that essentially created community-sized space suits with "centrifugal pseudo-gravity along long axes", packed for launch and inflated upon orbit. The modules were to be identical and assembled from the inside out "in a shirt sleeve environment". It was radical and completely opposite to NASA's baseline conception – rigid platforms of different sizes and shapes, delivered in pieces, and assembled in orbit requiring hundreds or even thousands of hours of spacewalks with specialized tools and training required to achieve habitability. This one innovation alone would carve billions of dollars and years of development off the project…and there were more. As Lowell pointed out in his presentation, "Time [not risk] is the enemy." Federal R&D programs tend to grow "barnacles", he argued, and speedboats become barges over ten to fifteen years. He thundered, "There has *never* been a successful twenty-five to thirty year federal technology program." He was, and still is right (although the International Space Station may be the exception that proves the rule.)

Lowell is an outsized man with an outsized ego, looking vaguely like a mature Henry the VIII. He was neither shy nor secretive about his ideas and was therefore happy to share his thoughts and designs with peers (although I suspect he regarded the true group that fit the designation of his "peers" to be very small indeed). Lowell's openness meant that we could talk informally about his plan with members of the community without concern for protecting his ideas or necessarily associating the Space Council with them. We did so first to validate the first order feasibility and also to protect a case in which the Council might consider the Livermore proposal as an adjunct or peer competitor to that offered by NASA. But we still hadn't seen NASA's work and we wanted to offer the benefit of the doubt to NASA that the Agency would step up to the real challenge that they faced. We hoped for the best, but prepared for the worst.

On November 15, 1989, two days before the Space Council was to convene to consider the NASA 90-day study, the Policy Implementation and Review Committee (PIRC) of the Space Council met to get our first formal look at the NASA plan. Admiral Truly presented the work and our worst fears were instantly realized. NASA had prepared an architectural outline for meeting the President's challenge that first completed the Space Station exactly as it had already been planned and programmed and next called for the development of a cargo version of the Space Shuttle, dubbed "Shuttle C". Then, and only then, would work on human exploration begin by adding on to the completed Space Station to create a transit node for the launch of missions to the Moon and Mars. And as to "alternatives", there were five options, labeled A through E. As the National Academy of Sciences were later to report to the Vice President in their assessment of the plan, "The reference approaches in NASA's 90-day study are largely variations on a theme and have certain features in common. They depend on heavy lift vehicles (the shuttle and shuttle C) to Low Earth Orbit (LEO), and on the Space Station Freedom for assembly in LEO and as a transportation node.... The approaches described in the NASA study are relatively low in risk, in that each would proceed in methodical steps after earlier steps have been proven and after scientific and engineering questions inherent in the architecture are answered."[13]

We had some important choices to make, and to make quickly. One of the members of the Council staff walked into my office just an hour after the meeting with the committee of Space Council deputies and said that the Office of Public Affairs from NASA just called to say that Admiral Truly was planning a press conference Friday afternoon, after the Space Council meeting to discuss the 90-day study. He invited me to attend the conference with him.

III.

WHO'S THE BOSS?

"I fired MacArthur because he wouldn't respect the authority of the president. I didn't fire him because he was a dumb son of a bitch, although he was."
Harry S. Truman

After consultations with the Vice President, The Office of Management and Budget, the Office of Science and Technology Policy, and the NSC we decided that we were left with only one option to preserve the basic approach adopted by the White House all along. We would provide the NASA 90-day study *and* the Livermore study together at the Council meeting, implicitly giving them equal weight and equal consideration…and we would let the media know beforehand that we were doing so. The collision with NASA that we had tried to avoid, that we had done everything in our power to avert, was at hand.

To this day, I remain mystified at the incredible misreading of the times, temperament, and trends that NASA stubbornly embraced with their secretive 90-day study. Was it possible that they thought they could circumvent the clear direction of the White House and make it stick? Could they – with their industry base so desperately looking to new opportunities to offset the "peace dividend" cliff that might reduce the technology base of the United States by a factor of two – have so totally misread the situation? Could they have completely misread their brother and sister departments and agencies that were also looking at radical reductions in their missions, seeking out new opportunities to preserve their technology base?

I called my old friend John Tuck, undersecretary of the Department of Energy, to make certain he knew what we planned to do the next day and that he and Admiral Watkins were okay with the plan. John was close to Senator Howard Baker during the early eighties and had held the position of Secretary for the Majority in the Senate during my years there. He was one of the people in the administration I knew I could trust to give me sound political *and* policy advice. John told me that he and Admiral Watkins were not only aware of the Livermore work, but in fact were delighted that the Council would give it consideration. He said we could count on him and Secretary Watkins for support of what the President and Vice President wanted to do. I know this may sound somewhat surprising, but as I had learned over the nine months that I had been in the administration, this seemingly fundamental attribute, to be counted on to fully support the President and Vice President, could not be uniformly applied to all members of the administration.

I called Don Rice, Secretary of the Air Force, another old friend. Don had been the CEO and President of the Rand Corporation when I was in graduate school at the Rand Graduate Institute. Don was close to Senator Wilson, who sponsored Don's appointment to the Air Force position. I told Don of the Space Council's plans. He felt our approach was totally appropriate and wondered out loud, "What on earth is NASA thinking?" I heard similar reactions from Reggie Bartholomew at State and Allen Bromley at OSTP.

My call to Dick Truly was less than cheerful. He was polite but quiet, clearly unhappy with what the Council planned for the meeting the next day. He asked, "Shall we release our report as planned?" I told him that the matter of what to release would be discussed at the Council meeting and a decision would be made at that time. Two hours later, the NASA press conference was cancelled.

The day of the Space Council meeting was greeted by a prominent story on the federal page of the *Washington Post* written by Kathy Sawyer, then the beat reporter for science and technology. The story, headlined "QUAYLE TO GIVE NASA COMPETITION ON IDEAS FOR SPACE EXPLORATION", laid out what the White House expected from the exploration initiative in terms of technology development and a new national objective harnessing the innovative might of the entire American technology base. It described the meeting that was to take place that day and noted that "two, not one, plan would be before the members of the Council today."[14]

As we filed into the Cordell Hull Room of the Old Executive Office Building there was a palpable tension in the air. The Cordell Hull Room, named after Franklin Roosevelt's Secretary of State, the Nobel Peace Prize winner and "father of the United Nations", is an interesting mix of old and new. The room itself had been restored to turn-of-the-century splendor during the Reagan administration, as had the rest of the Old Executive Office Building. A massive carved oak meeting table in the center of the room could easily seat twenty. The wood paneled walls were adorned with ornate patterns of paint, gilt, and wainscoting, and early American scenes from the Hudson Valley School of painting hung on several walls. Yet the Hull Room was the most modern and secure room in the OEOB. It had been completely outfitted as a second "situation room" for the White House, with state of the art telecommunications systems, including new video links with the various command centers around the city and around the globe. With the flip of a switch, panels in the walls could disappear, revealing large television monitors to conference with the Departments of Defense and State, the major global US combat commands, the CIA and other members of the intelligence community. The set up was identical to the situation room in the basement of the West Wing, only larger. On this day, the Hull Room functioned as a mini-cabinet room. Members of the Council and their staffs quietly consulted with one another as the principals took their seats. Greetings among the members of the Council were friendly but subdued. When Admiral Truly arrived he smiled broadly and shook each member's hand with vigor.

The Vice President entered the room – preceded, as is customary, by several Secret Service agents who thrust open the door of the conference room, looked around for a second or two, and then propped open the inner door through which Quayle breezed into the room. The assemblage stood as Quayle entered the room and made the rounds of the standing department and agency heads. Quayle then started the meeting by noting important developments since the last Space Council meeting in October. First among these was the issuance of a National Space Policy signed by President Bush on November 2. This National Space Policy was signed as National Security Directive #30 *and*

National Space Policy Directive #1. Quayle commented that this policy, and the President's decision to initiate National Space Policy Directives as formal mechanisms of Executive Order, was a testimony to the importance the President placed on space in this administration. Quayle then turned his attention to the Defense Appropriations Bill which was working its way through Congress and, in particular, funding for the National Aerospace Plane (NASP).

The Council had closely monitored the progress of the National Aerospace Plane. NASP was a joint project between NASA and DoD with the goal of providing a reusable single-stage-to-orbit vehicle that would offer flexible, affordable, and safe transit to and from low earth orbit. The NASP would support a multitude of national missions, from scientific inquiry, to on-orbit satellite repair and retrofit, to real-time reconnaissance and force application. It was a bold and aggressive leap based on a series of new materials and technologies that offered a solution to what had stood and remains a canon of orbital mechanics: the "Tsiolkovsky Formula". Posited almost fifty years earlier by a Russian school-teacher, Konstantin Tsiolkovsky, the formula mathematically demonstrates that only multi-staged rockets can escape Earth's gravity. Simply put, Tsiolkovsky proved that the energy contained in propellants necessary to achieve escape velocity could not overcome the total weight of those propellants, the tanks necessary to hold them, and engines required to convert them into thrust energy at launch. Therefore, Tsiolkovsky argued, in order to achieve orbit, propellants converted to energy and expended, the tanks that hold them, and the engines that consume them must all be jettisoned and replaced by entirely new ones – hence, *staged* space flight. There is no magic formula for the number of stages – they have ranged from two to five – but there had been no escaping the fact of staged orbital flight.

The NASP was designed to circumvent the consequences of the Tsiolkovsky Formula by using a trick employed by airplanes; namely, using oxygen in the atmosphere as the oxidizer for the chemical creation of thrust. What airplanes carry as fuel is actually only one portion of the chemical thrust equation; the other part, oxygen, is pulled from the atmosphere, compressed, and then mixed with the fuel to create combusted thrust. The problem for space launch is that, as you rapidly ascend, the air, or more properly, the oxygen contained in it, gets thinner and thinner to the point where there isn't enough to be extracted and combined with the fuel. As a consequence, rockets need to carry all of their oxidizer with them from the very beginning, usually in its densest and heaviest form, liquid, making the rocket and its tanks very, very heavy. The NASP was based on the utilization of a new invention: the "aerospike engine". The aerospike engine would not only be able to convert itself from a jet engine to a rocket engine while in flight, using only the oxygen available from the atmosphere, but it also utilized an innovative design that essentially turned the engine inside out, substituting a virtual nozzle for the concentration and expulsion of thrust without the weight of physical nozzles. Thus, the NASP didn't need the liquid oxygen of a conventional rocket engine. It would need only a fraction of the total oxygen typically consumed in space flight, and by being assembled with extraordinarily light, strong, and thermally insulated new materials, it would achieve a thrust-to-weight ratio that could lift the entire vehicle from the ground to orbit and back again without jettisoning any-thing *except* thrust. One set of tanks and one set of engines, completely reusable. It wasn't exactly "warp drive", but it wasn't the V-2 either.

The NASA appropriation for the joint NASP program currently stood at $60 million, down from a request of $127 million. The DoD appropriations for the project stood at $285 million in the House and nothing in the Senate. This is an all too frequent problem with otherwise desirable joint projects: the various authorizing and appropriating committees of different departments and agencies can "game the system" in order to ease the financial burden from one appropriated account onto another. The NASA appropriators were trying to shift the financial burden of the NASP from NASA to DoD. This is pre-cisely the kind of matter that the Council was created to address. That day the Vice President was able to report that, while the Defense Appropriation Bill had yet to be passed in final form, the committee chairman had assured him that the NASP would be funded at the level requested by the administration. This was a significant accomplishment and reflected an important partnership between Congress and the administration on space infrastructure investment.

At this point, Quayle turned to the matter at hand. He explained that the Council was to hear a report from NASA on their ideas for architectural and technology alternatives for implementing the President's call for a new space exploration initiative. This work was to be "a starting point, not a baseline plan," and on each Council member's seat there was a report, prepared by the Energy Department and Livermore Laboratory, providing an alternative set of approaches. He said that he knew NASA had worked hard on its report and that all appreciated its efforts. Quayle said that he wanted the advice of the Council on whether we should make either or both of these inputs publically available, and asked that each department and agency prepare a review of what they were about to hear and read. With that, he turned the briefing over to Dick Truly.

Truly's presentation that day was straightforward and factual, with much less of the assuredness that had been on display two days earlier at the PIRC meeting (at one point at the PIRC meeting, in direct response to a question about alternatives, Admiral Truly said, "Look, if we are going to the Moon and on to Mars with human beings, this is more or less the way we are going to do it"). As at the PIRC, cost was estimated and presented as not thoroughly validated; wide ranges were offered. At the core of the proposal were the five alternative scenarios presented before, and there was no mention of new technology initiatives that could "change the game" in terms of cost, schedule, or performance.

The Secretary of Energy, James Watkins, former Chief of Naval Operations, asked to speak first. Watkins is a formidable man, tall, trim with a square jaw, sharp features, and an aquiline nose. He is an imposing figure with a friendly and affable manner. Well educated and articulate, Admiral Watkins was the soul of serious thought and inspired confidence on the bridge, in the inner sanctum of the Joint Chiefs of Staff, and in the Cabinet room. Watkins began by thanking his colleague and friend, Dick Truly, for an important and thorough presentation; he said that he knew it represented an enormous amount of work and years of experience. He then proceeded to make an impassioned case for making this new era of exploration a clear challenge to America's entire technology base to drive down costs, advance schedules, reduce risks, and, in fact, create a technological imperative to reach beyond our planet. He said that the benefits to the American public and the world at large would be incalculable and would last for generations. The challenges in the post-Cold War world would be energy, climate, sustaining a habitable planet, and international cooperation for global problems. All of these, he said, "are within the scope and purpose of this new initiative." He argued that all parochial ideas and positions must be set aside in pursuit of this important new goal.

"At the first meeting of his cabinet," Watkins reminded the Council, "President Bush charged us to 'think big' and 'challenge the system'. If this is not the time and opportunity to do so, I can think of nothing other worthy of the charge. I understand what you are trying to do, Mr. Vice President. This is a Strategic Defense Initiative that will work. We have no constraint under the Anti-Ballistic Missile Treaty, and if our policy and strategy are in line with our technology, American resources will respond and succeed."

Then, one by one, members of the Council concurred, associating themselves with Secretary Watkins's remarks and pledging to offer the support and efforts of their departments and agencies to achieve the goals and vision of the President. Secretary of the Air Force Don Rice said, "I completely agree with Jim Watkins. This is an SDI that will work."

Dick Darman, however, was a voice of caution. He said that, while he was in complete agreement with Secretary Watkins and the vision the Vice President had offered, he was concerned that we not cavalierly cast aside the foundation we had already built. He said that too radical a change in course could risk the support we needed in Congress. For example, if we were to abruptly abandon or substantially scale back the Freedom Space Station, we would not only leave many international partners in the lurch and the industrial team in limbo, but we would also risk losing the Congressional coalition that supported human spaceflight. He said we were entering dangerous waters that required very careful navigation. He pledged his support at OMB in providing resources within the other departments and agencies, particularly DoD and DoE, in order to contribute to the initiative, but he said we also needed to be clear that this was not a slow dissolution of NASA, but rather a marshalling of the entire federal technology enterprise towards a new national goal with implications not only for space science and exploration, but also for our future economic health, technological vitality, and national security interests. He said that our financial ramp up for this initiative needed to be careful and steady as we built support in the nation, the Congress, and the international community. He turned to Dick Truly and said, "You need to get with this program because you will be on the front lines of explaining what we are doing. Secretary

Watkins has got it just right: we must leave our parochial concerns behind as we embark on a new course...and NASA must be the most committed, the most vocal in support of it."

The Vice President said, "This has been an important meeting for the Council, and for the future." He wanted each member to review the materials presented and then report back to the Council on their findings and how they planned to contribute to this new initiative.

IV.

FROM BARE KNUCKLES
TO BEAR HUGS

On the cold afternoon of November 9, 1989, Gunther Schabowski, the East German Minister of Propaganda, weary from a late night return to Berlin and confused by a guidance memo he had just received from the new Kreunz government of East Germany, held a press conference in his offices. The briefing was about the mounting pattern of large scale, unauthorized emigration to the West from several of the Warsaw Pact nations and East Germany's response to mounting pressure to follow suit. To the amazement of all, Schabowski, rather than announcing a very limited program of brief visits between East and West Germans, abruptly announced that there would be no limitations upon East Germans migrating to West Germany whatsoever, effective immediately. Within hours, tens of thousands of East Germans pushed towards the famous "Check Point Charlie" between East and West Germany and, in the ensuing chaos, the border guards, without instruction and left to their own initiative, opened the gates that had stood as a symbol of isolation, repression, and fear since 1961. The Berlin Wall had fallen.

Reports of massive emigration from East to West through Czechoslovakia and Hungary had circulated all that fall, but the absolutely stunning images seen worldwide of thousands of East Germans pouring through the Brandenburg Gates, standing on the forbidden Wall, and embracing their western brethren were the undeniable proof of what we had thought would never happen: the end of the Cold War. Reports of the opening circulated throughout the day, but it wasn't until later that evening, when the networks broke in to report the story and show the astounding images of people standing on top of the Berlin Wall, madly waving flags of the Republic of Germany, pounding away at the bricks and mortar of the dreaded Wall with every device imaginable, that the reality of the event sank in. People were crying and embracing and literally dancing in the streets. My wife and I sat in stunned silence in front of the television. I worked in the White House for God's sake and I had no idea that this was coming. We spontaneously began to cry – it was simply so overwhelming. We decided to wake the children, who groggily walked down the hallway and plopped in front of the television as we told them what was happening. I know we didn't come close to capturing the real significance of the moment, and I know the children had little sense of what was going on. But it didn't matter – this was simply so momentous that we thought they should witness it firsthand.

The newspapers covered the events on page one the next day, but resisted the triumphalism that one might have expected given the climactic events. The *New York Times* led with "A Jubilant Horde" and "East Berliners Explore Land Long Forbidden." Yet despite all the coverage, there was scarcely one quote from a Bush administration official.[15] The *Wall Street Journal* got one quote from President Bush, who called the event "a dramatic happening," simply adding, "I'm elated." On the editorial page, the *Journal* published Ronald Reagan's famous speech calling on Mr. Gorbachev to "tear down this wall" and, just below that, celebrated "the removal of a scar that has so long defaced Europe."[16]

Years later, President Bush recounted the events of that day in his book, A World Transformed. He explained his somewhat muted public response that day. "As Brent [Scowcroft] pointed out, this was not a time to gloat about what many in the West would interpret as a defeat for Gorbachev." [17]

The media and some in Congress took the President to task for his lack of euphoria over the fall of the Wall that day; however, it was clear that his response was in fact the result of careful consideration.

"On the day the Wall opened," Bush later wrote, "Gorbachev sent messages to Kohl warning him to stop talking of reunification, and cabled me urging that I not overreact. He worried that the demonstrations might get out of control with 'unforeseen consequences' and he asked for understanding. This was the first time Gorbachev had clearly indicated genuine anxiety about events in Eastern Europe.... It was as if he suddenly realized the serious implications of what was going on. As I read the cable I again thought of the posturing by many members of Congress".[18]

Clearly, the fall of the Berlin Wall was more than a metaphor for the disintegration of the Soviet Bloc; it was, in fact, a foreshadowing of the collapse of the entire Soviet Union and the Communist regime at its core. The risks of miscalculation at this crucial moment were enormous. All Americans, indeed everyone around the world, owes an enormous debt of gratitude to President Bush for his steady and calm reaction and leadership on this day and on all the days that were to follow as the world transformed.

The next day at the White House was surreal. All anyone could talk of was the unbelievable chain of events and the dramatic scenes of thousands of Germans joyfully poring over the border into the arms of awaiting West Berliners. It was like the final moments of an intense sporting competition, when the reality of victory sinks in for one of the competitors: at that moment, it becomes clear that neither time nor chance can reverse the outcome on the field for the vanquished. There was almost shocked amazement on the expression of everyone. No doubt about it, the Soviet Union as we had known it for decades would be no more – only the "how" and precisely "when" were in question.

After the fall of the Berlin Wall, the winter of 1989 was a period of accelerating decline in the Soviet Union. Eastern European countries began to distance themselves from the Soviet Union, politically, economically, and socially. As we were later to find, resources within Russia were becoming scarce and cutbacks in government spending were severe, and nothing, including the space program was spared. Earlier in the year, President Gorbachev had given a speech in which he said, "Expenditures in the [military and civil] space program have already been partially cut.... We must seek more possibilities in this direction."[19] As funds for the prized Soviet military and civil space program were sacrificed to provide the basic necessities of food, energy, and shelter for

Russian citizens, there could be no doubt that matters had become serious, if not dire, indeed.

President Bush later noted that, in his preparations for his first summit with Gorbachev in early December at Malta, one CIA analyst paper he read had concluded that "Gorbachev's economic reforms were doomed to failure, and that his political changes were beginning to cause problems he might not be able to control. It argued that the reforms were strong enough to disrupt the Soviet system, but not strong enough to give the Soviet people the benefits of a market economy. Based on those conclusions, some people in the NSC began to speculate that Gorbachev might be headed for a crisis which could force him to crack down in the Soviet Union to maintain order, or might even force him from power."[20]

President Bush weighed the policy alternatives in the run up to Malta and the White House staff worked on providing not only analysis and insights, but also concrete ideas about the agenda for the summit. On November 29, I wrote a memorandum for the Vice President outlining options for space exploration cooperation that reflected our "new thinking".

"You may wish to bring to the President's attention," I noted, "the fact that President Gorbachev has raised the issue of 'going to Mars together' at the last two Reagan summits. Present cable traffic indicates that President Gorbachev may raise this issue again at Malta. A wide range of options reflecting several levels of cooperation with the Soviet Union is under study [by the Space Council] for the President's consideration early next year. These initial studies can provide a basis for options if Mr. Gorbachev broaches the subject of closer cooperation or if the President chooses to initiate the subject at Malta."

In the memorandum, I specifically proposed three alternative options that I believed were supportable in the current context: 1) agreement to study jointly long-term human exploration; 2) agreement to initiate technical exchanges for near-term cooperation on issues such as crew rescue, space debris, and emergency communications between space centers, all in anticipation of later exploration cooperation; and 3) agreement to immediately begin planning for cooperative unmanned precursor missions to the Moon and Mars in the 1990s, followed by joint human exploration activities. I shared this memo with Brent Scowcroft and Condi Rice at the NSC, both of whom agreed with its findings and felt that it should be "on the table" with the President and the summit team. So it was included in the briefing book for Malta.

Often summits take on a life and momentum of their own, and the Malta summit was no different. As it turned out, a crisis in the Philippines, bad weather and high seas in the straits of Gibraltar where the two leaders were to meet on war ships, and a full agenda on Eastern Europe and Central America resulted in no discussions of space cooperation. As President Bush later reported in A World Transformed, President Gorbachev said, "The Soviet Union is ready to no longer regard the United States as an adversary and is ready to state that our relationship is cooperative." Bush continued, "It was time to think beyond the arms race. He [Gorbachev] complained that while the Soviet Union had switched to a defensive military doctrine, the United States and NATO had not yet changed their doctrine."[21]

This matter of doctrinal shift was on the mind of President Bush as early as the evening of the fall of the Berlin Wall: "The big question I ask myself is how we capitalize on these changes? And what does the Soviet Union have to do before we make dramatic changes in our defense structure? The bureaucracy answer will be, do nothing big, and wait and see what happens. But I don't want to miss an opportunity.... The budget process is crunching defense, but I'm telling our people that we must challenge the defense system, and go back to demand new studies, so we can see what bold [arms control] proposals can really benefit mankind and yet keep the West secure. As the changes happen, I am absolutely convinced that there will be declining support for [defense expenditures] all around Europe."[22]

The Space Exploration Initiative was tailor-made to address the presidents' gut instincts at this moment in history: to step away from the Cold War, and yet, for the sake of future economic vitality and the transformed world, preserve the vital technology base that had been created to wage it. We were doing all in our power to put the matter in this context and to this end. We were fighting an entrenched NASA bureaucracy and some in Congress intent on staying in the past, locked into Cold War thinking, and protecting bureaucratic turf. Yet many in the administration and in the larger space community understood the President and Vice President and were actively helping realize the vision they offered. So in the winter of 1989 and the following spring we assembled a coalition for a new space enterprise, but we confronted an equally formidable coalition committed to the status quo. Remarkably, and perhaps not coincidentally, at almost the same time, a coalition of powerful Russian politicians, academic elites, and military-industrial bosses were considering the same set of facts, the same outlook for the future, and the same ideas for preserving a technology base in a post-Cold War Russia. They too were also confronting powerful internal obstacles. Like two star-crossed lovers in a Shakespearean tragedy, with miscues, misinterpretations, bad relatives, and self-serving surrogates, our governments were off and on again, and plans for space cooperation were not always high priority. All too often one partner would become enthusiastic about this cooperation only to find the other distracted. Then later, when that partner warmed to cooperation, the other would cool. But by the early months of 1990, our plans for space cooperation seemed to be getting closer to taking the center stage of policy and politics on both sides.

V.

HEIRS OF KOROLOV LOOK
TO THE WEST

"In Russia the breakup of the Soviet Union led to political and economic chaos. Although Russia's MIR space station and other historic achievements dating back to Sputnik were a source of national pride, the Russian space program was financially starved and its future was uncertain."
Susan Eisenhower, *Partners in Space*

In 1994, Russian physicist, leading academic, director of the Space Research Institute, and former member of the Supreme Soviet, Roald Sagdeev wrote a revealing autobiography, *The Making of a Soviet Scientist*.[23] In this important work, Sagdeev recounts the last few years of the Soviet Union and the internal struggles of the Soviet space enterprise as it faced perestroika, glasnost, and eventually the dissolution of the Soviet Union. It is a story of intrigue and power politics within the teetering Soviet regime, as important industrial barons, elite academicians, and political operatives began to jockey for position, influence, and precious resources within what could only be dimly perceived as a post-Soviet Russia.

I first met Roald Sagdeev in the spring of 1990, when we were in the midst of conceiving and planning what would become the Shuttle-Mir program, a cooperative effort between the US and the Soviet Union to fly Russian cosmonauts aboard the US Space Shuttle in exchange for the long-duration flight of US astronauts aboard the Russian space station Mir. Roald is a gentle and soft spoken man with a manner and style that invites serious discussion and thought. He has a wry sense of humor, and a legendary intellect that is disarming. He speaks carefully, raising controversial ideas and thoughts innocently and with a certain distance – perhaps the result of a long life spent in the inner sanctum of the famously capricious Soviet elite.

In 1990, Roald married Susan Eisenhower, granddaughter of President Dwight D. Eisenhower, and moved to the United States, where he took a teaching position at the University of Maryland. At that time and still today, he is very knowledgeable of activities in Moscow and remains well connected with his former Russian colleagues.

Roald's extraordinary autobiography and his description of the events, perceptions, and initiatives within the complex Soviet space community unfolding at the exact moment we were initiating significant changes in our own program, is instructive. His observations provide a rich backdrop to what I experienced firsthand in the period from December 1989 until the fall of 1990.

As Roald recounts, Soviet Chairman Mikhail Gorbachev was a contemporary of his who attended Moscow State University in political science while Roald was winning prizes in the physics department. Gorbachev became an influential party boss in the Stravpol region and eventually a member of the Central Committee, charged with reviving the Soviet agriculture sector. Gorbachev's rapid rise in what Roald describes as the Soviet "gerontocracy" was nothing short of miraculous, a combination of personal talent and charm and the rapid succession of aging leaders in the 1980s that left the Soviet Union somewhat adrift. Gorbachev was a reformer from the start, sponsoring the ill-fated "prohibition" and "vodka moratorium" of 1985 and quickly turning his attention to international security and military buildup.[24] As Roald puts it, "Outside the understandable general strategic considerations, Gorbachev wanted the chance to reduce the future military budget as part of his program for the economic revival of the country."[25] But at the same time, Gorbachev was convinced that science and technology were areas that could contribute significantly to economic recovery. In fact, one of his first initiatives was "an intensified and accelerated path to rebuilding the economy with an emphasis on the greater role of science and high technology."[26]

Gorbachev's complex view of reform required an international cadre of informal ambassadors to explain the nuanced policy thrusts of "new thinking" in the context of "old habits". For example, arms control, and in particular reaffirmation of the ABM Treaty and its focus on space-based weaponry, was advanced at the same time as space exploration, prestige demonstrations (like the Buran and Energia rockets), and space cooperation. Sagdeev recounts a meeting of a large group of celebrities with the Central Committee, in mid-October 1985, in advance of the first summit in Geneva with President Reagan. They were told that "a special privileged list of people…were granted the right to meet foreigners: that is business people, journalists, and politicians who regularly asked for appointments and interviews. From now on we were told that we were entitled to say yes or no without the highest permission from the authorities…. [A] group of well defined people were given a special ticket for glasnost."[27]

By the winter of 1989, this special group of agents for reform had grown and many were making their way to Washington – and international space cooperation was chief among their agenda items.

———

As Susan Eisenhower carefully documents in her book *Partners in Space*, cooperation between the United States and the Soviet Union on space projects began to thaw in the later stages of the Reagan administration.[28] In 1987 an agreement was signed to authorize a five-year program of collaboration on space projects that reflected both Soviet interest in boosting its space prestige, as well as justifying its expenditures on space technology, and pressure on the US side to "decouple" space cooperation and arms control, deflect criticism about the offensive potential of SDI, and re-energize space activities after the tragic failure of the space shuttle Challenger.[29] Initially these low level discussions focused on joint scientific projects and did not include discussions of human spaceflight. That is, until the early winter of 1990, when I received a call from Sam Keller, the Deputy Associate Administrator for Space Science from NASA, asking to see me about his recent visit to Russia as part of the working group established under the 1987 agreement.

Sam is a tall, professorial kind of fellow with a casual and relaxed air; he had already spent over twenty years at NASA rising from a researcher at the Goddard Space Flight Center to Director of Administration and Management at headquarters, then to Associate Deputy Administrator for Space Science and Applications. He was the closest thing NASA had to a college provost: a scientist-turned-administrator, now back again to management, a steady and useful presence, always on the periphery of power. He had been relegated the assignment of representing NASA in the US-Soviet Space Working Group. He was of that cadre of US civil servants who make the most out of international assignments that others in the "mainstream" shun. He found a niche in the small and largely overlooked joint US-Soviet science committee created by Secretary of State George Shultz and Foreign Minister Edvard Shevardnadze in the mid-eighties each for their own largely domestic reasons.

Sam arrived at my office in the White House on that cold January morning with interesting news from his December trip to Moscow. It seemed that what had been advertised as a routine exchange between US and Soviet academic scientists about ongoing collaborative work on the atmosphere and oceans had turned into a summons by the powerful Chief of the Ministry of General Machine Building, Oleg Shishkin, to tour the Energia plant in Moscow – a first for a Westerner. Keller recounted his entry into this most secret of heavy machinery works and his tour of the plant. Shishkin personally escorted him around the facility, with numerous rockets, missiles, and spacecraft in various stages of assembly. Keller described the general condition of the facility and the level of activity. He thought it somewhat dilapidated by US standards and certainly unsafe, far below the standards of OSHA. Teams worked diligently, but there was a clear excess of capacity in the plant, indicating a lull in production probably due to a significant downturn in work. He said Shishkin was intensely interested in how NASA and the Defense Department regarded Soviet space technology and whether or not we considered them "on par" with our own or merely "second rate". He wanted to know what Sam thought about the prospects of serious cooperation, including in the area of human spaceflight. He offered that the Soviets were eager to work with us and that they had a great deal to offer to President Bush's new space exploration initiative.

To his credit, Sam courageously pushed Shishkin by asking directly whether or not their interest in cooperation was driven largely by money. He asked, "Are you really interested in cooperation, or simply the hard currency that you might be able to extract from the United States?"

At this Shishkin took great umbrage, telling Keller, "We have a space program that we are completely capable of carrying out. So do you. We are only interested in cooperation for cooperation's sake." He then asked Keller to extend a personal invitation to Admiral Truly to come to Moscow "to see for himself". Shishkin promised to show Truly things never before seen by the West and to demonstrate that the excellence of Soviet space technology and the advancements in their capabilities could greatly reduce the time and cost of an exploration initiative.

As skeptical as Keller was about the motivations of Shishkin, I was equally skeptical about the motivations of NASA. Clearly Shishkin was trying to place himself at the center of any potential space cooperation with the United States and so were Keller and NASA with regard to Russia. Roald Sagdeev's description of the internal struggles within the Soviet space program at this time placed Shishkin and the other "greedy space barons" at odds with the "new ambassadors" of the Gorbachev regime over the true intent of space cooperation; for science, economic advancement, and glasnost, or for cash, control, and power. The academicians and the "celebrities" Roald described as having a free hand in meetings and encounters with the West contrasted with Shishkin's inability to travel to the United States and thereby directly pressing his case to US officials for the Ministry's primacy in future space projects. This then, was the root cause of Shishkin's opportunistic "hijack" of the NASA delegation that day in Moscow and NASA's eager interest in controlling the agenda. Both had miscalculated: Shishkin had no way of knowing that the space exploration initiative had such high-level attention in the United States that the White House and the Department of State were asserting their dominance in what was shaping to be a whole new thrust in US foreign policy and direction for the space program. Further, he had no way of knowing that NASA, which had been given benign but distinctly limited leadership in managing small and low-level science demonstrations in the past, would be placed in the role of implementer of this new and bold round of cooperation. He also couldn't have known that NASA was, at best, a reluctant participant in substantially reorganizing the baseline space program to incorporate Soviet participation, and that the Agency was highly motivated to manage any potential cooperation as they were doing with other international partnerships on the Space Station program: at arms length.[30]

Several days after Sam's visit, the President's science advisor, Allan Bromley, dropped by my office to provide me with a letter he had just received from the Soviet Ambassador, Yuri Dubinin. Bromley was a genial man with an academic posture. At the time he was sixty-three years old and looked in all ways like the twin brother of the Wizard of Oz. He had come from the faculty of Yale and was well dressed in university tweeds, wore a bow tie daily, and had a shock of white hair and bushy white eyebrows that energetically responded to his mood and point of view. He always seemed to me to be somewhat adrift in the political pull and haul of the White House, and he routinely frustrated his colleagues, especially Dick Darman, with his flexibility on matters of policy. This was especially true on the issue of climate change, where his views and positions seemed to change, well, with the weather.

Bromley had come to see me carrying with him the letter from Dubinin. This letter recounted a meeting the ambassador had had with Bromley the week before and it enumerated a list of space ideas, including a timeline for each: from 1990 to 1992, an American space flight on board the Soviet space station Mir, timed to coincide with the fifteenth anniversary of the Apollo-Soyuz project; from 1995 to 1997, a Soviet cosmonaut space flight on the manned orbital Space Station Freedom; by 2005, a joint Soviet-US manned mission to the Moon; and from 2015 to 2017, a joint Soviet-US manned mission to Mars. Dubinin was asking for Bromley's help in establishing a dialogue between NASA and the Ministry of General Machine Building. Bromley seemed positively flummoxed by the matter, sensing that he was drifting into national security and foreign policy matters of which he clearly wanted no part. In fairness, Bromley was not much interested in space. He was a particle physicist and was most intently interested in the Super Conducting Super Collider project, enjoying mightily his role as ambassador to the science community and shying away as a general matter from controversial policy issues. My sense is that he was more than happy to hand off this particular issue and, when I told him that we were fully engaged in the issue, he retreated with relief to the offices of OSTP (the Office of Science and Technology Policy.)

A week later, the Soviet Ambassador asked for a meeting with the Vice President. Ambassador Dubinin routinely checked the pulse of the administration on everything from Eastern Europe, to NATO, to SDI, with the Vice President, because of Quayle's recent service in the Senate and his more conservative views on the Soviet Union. Dubinin usually focused particularly on the matter of trade, yet on this day he focused on space exploration and potential cooperation. He asked the Vice President to authorize NASA to engage in discussions with Shishkin. The Vice President said that he welcomed the initiative and that the administration was already looking at ideas as part of our new space exploration initiative. He described the National Space Council as the center of all US space policy and explained its role of coordination and policy formulation. He said he was aware that the Soviet government and its agents were trying different routes into the administration to explore cooperation. He told Dubinin, "You have come to the right place finally; we are the ones that will address this issue."

While this was welcome news to Dubinin, it left him without the real answer he sought and put him in an uncomfortable position. Dubinin was carrying the water for the "space baron" Shishkin, whose power inside Russia flowed from the military and the politburo; while Shishkin was part of the Gorbachev regime, he was not completely onboard with perestroika and glasnost thinking. His enterprise was suffering under the limitations of Soviet financial exhaustion and Gorbachev's initiative to demilitarize; he recognized that new possibilities for openness might mean new opportunities for his starving empire, but his sympathies and loyalties lay with the hard liners who were growing skeptical of Gorbachev and his perceived weakness. He therefore sought a partner in the United States who was just below the Presidential or ministerial level, who could comfortably pair with his ambitions, and potentially pay his bills: NASA was the perfect target. In his mind, why not? The President had said that he was leading the United States toward a new era of space exploration – and, of course, the country would follow. He said that he wanted new thinking about how to achieve the goals faster and cheaper without compromising safety. How could you do that more efficiently than by using existing, proven Soviet hardware? And the President said that he wanted international cooperation to establish a new means of global interaction. What better example than working with that old enemy, the Soviet Union?

The problem for the Russians was that using the Space Council as the agent for discussion, negotiation, and execution of space cooperation would require "presidential level" counterparts and involve bilateral tradeoffs on a broad range of issues at the highest levels — at ministerials for sure and at summits most likely. Shishkin couldn't pull that off while remaining loyal to his hard line sponsors in the Kremlin. His hope, therefore, was to cut a deal with NASA independently and present the Gorbachev government with a *fait accompli*...and cash. He recognized the opening presented by the President's new space exploration initiative, but his only perceived play was through NASA. He believed he needed access to NASA and, ironically for him, the Space Council's interventions were impeding it. From our perspective, we had offered Dubinin and the Soviets an expedited and success-oriented invitation to work directly with the White House on future cooperation, outside the status quo thinking at NASA. We knew that, while NASA would eagerly undertake talks with the Soviets if allowed to, they wouldn't deviate an iota from the baseline Station-Shuttle model. After all, even when pressed to do so for the reward of bold, new exploration horizons utilizing new US resources and new US technology, they had balked and stalled; certainly they wouldn't change the baseline now to take advantage of using Soviet resources to "leapfrog" the timeline and budget.

The message to the ambassador seemed to be sinking in. In March 1990, Dubinin brought several academicians into the White House for meetings on space cooperation. Ossipian, Frolov, and Barsykov all carried similar messages: "Let's do something together, something big, something worthy of two super-powers." The Vice President participated in a few of these meetings and was growing increasingly concerned that we get beyond feel-good atmospherics and down to concrete proposals. One particular meeting in early March involved a lengthy and expansive vision by academician Frolov for joint US-Soviet science cooperation from education to industry; I remember Quayle looking at me in the middle of the rambling monologue and rolling his eyes. Ambassador Dubinin cut off Frolov after a time and said, "Let's work concrete proposals for the upcoming ministerials in May." He then informed the Vice President that he had personally spoken with Gorbachev about space cooperation and that Gorbachev was enthusiastically supportive of it and suggested that we include the topic at the White House summit in June.

He then said, "In a few days, the Soviet Union will announce that on March 12, for the first time ever, the People's Congress will hold an election for President. Presumably Gorbachev will be elected, but at the same time they will announce direct elections for President by citizens of the Soviet Union in the future and ownership of private property."

One week later, Gorbachev was indeed elected President by the Party Congress, but tensions in the Party and the government were beginning to show. In May, the Supreme Soviet became deadlocked over the election of the largely ceremonial post of Chairman: the Communist loyalists supported one candidate, the reformers supported Boris Yeltsin. In the end, Yeltsin won – a significant blow to Gorbachev's prestige and to the power and credibility of Party apparatchiks like Shishkin. Shortly thereafter, Yelstin resigned from the Communist Party and one year later was himself elected President; soon after that, a much more junior and relatively unknown administrator, Yuri Koptiev, replaced Shishkin.

The White House team was of one mind on the matter of Soviet cooperation in space: we were for it...under the right conditions. Condi Rice and Brent Scowcroft agreed to keep secret the Vice President's meeting with Dubinin and his offer to start a dialogue on long-term space cooperation. We told NASA that a visit to Moscow by Admiral Truly would be put on indefinite hold until the Council had an opportunity to address comprehensively the matter of international cooperation on the space exploration initiative. Reggie Bartholomew, Under-Secretary of State for International Affairs and confident of Secretary Jim Baker, was in complete agreement and we looked ahead to the Bush-Gorbachev summit in June and the Baker-Shevardnadze ministerials in May as potential opportunities to negotiate directly. The Space Council was working two tracks simultaneously: a formal interagency track on the matter of international cooperation for the new space exploration initiative, and a separate, secret track on specific US-Soviet initiatives to be pursued at the ministerial and Presidential level. Our most promising idea for immediate and direct cooperation was an exchange of astronauts and cosmonauts on the Space Shuttle and the Russian space station Mir. Our reasoning was simple: the National Academy of Sciences had argued that the most urgent need for establishing the viability of long-term human exploration of space, either long duration missions to the Moon or a manned expedition to Mars, was solid medical data on the effects of space flight on the human body. Short space shuttle missions were too limited to provide good data and we would have to wait years for the space station to be ready to house crews for months at a time. Putting US astronauts on Mir for months with full medical instrumentation could carve years off the exploration initiative and potentially obviate the need for a US space station altogether. Even the CIA confirmed that including Soviet cosmonauts in US astronaut training in Houston and flights on the shuttle would compromise very little in terms of technology. It was perfect. In the early spring of 1990, all things seemed possible – yet, unbeknownst to us, we were operating under false premises. The water in Gorbachev's own bathtub was beginning to boil.

The picture began to focus for me in April 1990, when Susan Eisenhower requested that I meet with her husband, Roald Sagdeev. I had never met Roald before, but Carl Sagan and Lou Friedman had told me about him and his departure from Russia; they both strongly recommended that I meet with him and hear his perspectives on developments in Russia and the Soviet space complex. I remember Roald coming to my office in the middle of a busy day on Wednesday, April 4. We were in the midst of interacting with Congress on the President's budget request for FY91 and preparing a series of National Space Policy Directives implementing the space exploration initiative, a new approach to space launch, and rationalizing commercial space policy, all while coordinating with the NSC, DoD and, State on the upcoming ministerials and the summit on arms control and potential space cooperation. I excused myself as Roald entered my office in the late afternoon and asked his permission to wolf down a sandwich while we talked.

Unlike the other Soviet academicians I had met, Roald spoke perfect English, got directly to the point, and took all my questions without hesitation. He was frank and candid about conditions in Russia and the struggles inside the space complex.

Roald started by telling me about Gorbachev's interest in space cooperation; he said that Gorbachev had been extremely high on a joint US-Soviet
mission to Mars for years and had mentioned it to President Reagan twice. In
the beginning, Gorbachev's reasoning had been that if he could get the United
States to commit to the big new expenditure for a Mars expedition, it would
hurt the US ability to complete SDI both financially and technically. Gorbachev
also recognized that such a mission would highlight space developments in the
Soviet Union which were a key part of the myth of Soviet supremacy, or at least
parity, with the United States. Roald said that all that had changed, however,
with the collapse of the Soviet economy. The space program had lost favor in
the government and was seen as a vestige of the then discredited Breshnev era.
Gorbachev, who believed in the need for economic revival and a growing technology sector, now desperately needed space cooperation as a means to provide
independent impetus for proceeding with the space program at all. Ironically,
the linkage between space cooperation and technology and economic development was clearly at work on both sides.

Roald told me that Gorbachev was coming under significant pressure
from the hard liners in the military and Communist Party for weakness
in dealing with the Balkan states. I asked him why so many different players from the Soviet Union, seemingly unconnected from one another, were
seeking audience with the administration to talk about space cooperation. It
was as if every contact was the first. He told me that the turmoil between
the Academy and the Ministry of General Machine Building over the space
enterprise was manifesting itself in positioning for change inside Russia and
that good, high level contacts in the United States space community regarding new projects would be useful and important status symbols − and lev-
erage points − when the change came. I asked who among the players we
should work with; he replied, "Only those directly in contact with Gorbachev
himself."

We talked hypothetically about a number of potential areas of cooperation. Roald asked if I thought something could be accomplished at the summit
in June and I replied that it was conceivable, but that lots of work would be
needed and it depended largely on the progress in other areas outside the scope
of the space program. Roald mentioned a variety of ideas, including global envi-

ronmental monitoring and data sharing. He said that Minister Shishkin was desperate for cash and was very eager for a deal. I also mentioned some ideas, including a Shuttle-Mir exchange program. Roald locked onto that option right away, noting that it was "practical, useful and quickly implementable". I asked him what might be an impediment to making the project work.

"Beyond the internal politics in Russia, over which you have no control," he answered, "I would say it is important that you not emphasize too strongly that the lack of sophisticated medical protocols with Russian cosmonauts is the reason for astronaut travel to Mir. There are great sensitivities in the Russia space community about the Western perception of our technology. Advertising this initiative as a way to compensate for poor Soviet medical research will not make for success. I would recommend that you simply focus on the need to gather your own information on the effects of long term space flight on astronauts – not the fact that Soviet data is inadequate."

This made perfect sense to me. We had substantially run over the time allotted for the meeting, but Roald's insights were invaluable in helping me understand what was happening and, in retrospect, why the progress that we seemed to be making would come to a halt very soon.

VI.

THE HANDWRITING ON
THE WALL

By early 1990, the seeds planted in the Departments of Energy and Defense for participation in the planning and execution of the space exploration initiative were beginning to take root. In late November we had tasked DoE and DoD to review the NASA 90-day study and to report to the Council as soon as possible on their assessments and how they might be able to contribute to the effort. It was mid-January 1990 and word came that both DoD and DoE were ready to report. Around the same time, several leaders of the US aerospace industry – who had initially regarded the President's initiative with caution – came to our office to share their concerns about rapidly accelerating declines in defense spending and their interest in expanded space activities to partially offset the declines. It seemed that necessity had overcome their concerns about the potential wrath of their NASA customer for any deviations from agency orthodoxy. In the immortal words of Samuel Johnson, "Nothing so focuses a man's attention as the prospect of being hanged."

The first report came from the Defense Department and was presented by Lieutenant General Don Cromer, chief of the Air Force Space Division in Los Angeles. Cromer is a no-nonsense officer, tall and square jawed, an outstanding technologist with a sterling reputation as a manager of space programs. His straight-talking, clear-thinking style was perfect for DoD's response to the

NASA study. Cromer and his team of analysts came to the White House on January 24 and presented a two-hour, well thought out, serious and detailed report on the NASA study. No punches were pulled. DoD found the NASA report to be "pedestrian", lacking in technology alternatives, with neither the aggressive technology plans nor the management plans that could credibly bring it into being. Cromer said that DoD could contribute in many ways to the activity, from technology development to independent test and evaluation to accountability for specific mission tasks. He said that a realistic plan for streamlined management was the most urgent need of the initiative and recommended that DoD and DoE participate from the beginning. I asked General Cromer if he knew of any reason that the Space Division should not set up an organization to work on the space exploration initiative; he didn't. I turned to the representative of the Office of the Secretary of Defense and asked the same question. He replied with the same answer: there was no reason not to create a DoD entity to work on the initiative.

As they left, I asked General Cromer if he had briefed Admiral Truly and the NASA team on their work; he said they had. I asked, "How did Dick react?"

"He was not pleased," replied Cromer. He said that NASA agreed that some internal changes would need to be made, but that they didn't see DoD playing a role in the initiative, and they specifically pointed to the Space Act of 1958 as a bar to DoD involvement. We looked at each other with puzzlement since there were numerous collaborative activities already ongoing between NASA and DoD, not the least of which was the multibillion-dollar, jointly funded and jointly managed NASP launch program.

I called Secretary of Air Force Don Rice and congratulated him on the team's work and thanked him personally for his support. He reiterated his view that this was an important initiative and noted that the President's budget submission for FY91 – a submission that included a whopping 24% increase for NASA and an almost 12% increase for DoD space activities (in the context of an overall proposed 3% *reduction* in DoD spending) – was a clear message to the defense and aerospace team that he was serious about supporting US technology development and that DoD had an important role in this regard.

The next day Sig Hecker, Director of the Los Alamos Lab, came to my office to report on the DoE findings on the 90-day study. Sig is a spry Austrian with large wire-rimmed glasses and a neat moustache. He is quick witted and quick thinking, and a survivor in the arcane world of national laboratories. Admiral Watkins and John Tuck had given the NASA assignment to Los Alamos because its sister lab, Livermore, had submitted the earlier "unsolicited" proposal for returning to the Moon and then on to Mars and therefore would be "conflicted" in reporting on the NASA plan. Sig reported what was now increasingly becoming a consensus opinion: namely, that NASA had provided a very limited and unimaginative plan for space exploration, a plan that was predicated on completion of an existing baseline for Space Station Freedom as designed, without change, just as it had been pursuing prior to the President's announcement — as if the most far reaching space goal in twenty years contained nothing that might influence it.

Sig said that Los Alamos had lots of ideas about how to cut the cost, the schedule, and the risk of exploration, and that the labs had incredible capabilities to look at things like autonomous operations in space — which could be very usefully applied to the task and would also have incredible spinoff potential for everything from airplanes to manufacturing. He explained that Secretary Watkins had told him that he and his leadership team at DoE had looked to the future, to national projects that could utilize the kind of specialized expertise resident in the labs, and the only thing they saw on the horizon with the characteristics of a high-technology national effort was, in fact, the space program and, in particular, the space exploration initiative. They wanted to be part of that effort — not in a subordinate or marginal but, rather, a central role.

Clearly Defense and Energy were beginning to consider the future without a Cold War. For now, they stood atop technological empires with hundreds of thousands of skilled and dedicated workers, billions of dollars of industrial and research capacity, an army of scholars and researchers in all the major universities and institutes of the United States — all of it focused on cutting-edge technologies and new ideas. It was, without a doubt, the most extensive, advanced, and well-funded research and development enterprise in the history of the world, and only the most naïve or foolish person could not see what was at stake...and what was likely to follow.

As I left the White House that chilly night, after my meeting with Sig, I headed to the National Air and Space Museum to sit among the iconic

artifacts of almost ninety years of American air and space accomplishment
and power to listen to a giant of the American space enterprise, General Ben
Shriever, father of the ICBM and visionary of the military space program,
give the annual Werner Von Braun Lecture. It all was beginning to sink in
for me.

General Bernard Shriever was eighty years old in 1990, trim, fit, and still
sharp as ever. He was born in Bremen, Germany in 1910 and immigrated to
the United States in 1917. Bennie, as he was affectionately known to his friends,
had led the US development of Intercontinental Ballistic Missiles in the late
1950s and was widely regarded as the father of the military space program. He
looked and acted like Gary Cooper — a tall, quiet man of steel. That night he
recounted the history of the Air Force space program and the pivotal role it
played in the Cold War. He was unapologetic about the need for American
space superiority and he likened space and space forces to the great oceans and
the role of navies. He spoke of the Strategic Defense Initiative and the new
technologies that were being developed, and he particularly admired the "faster,
cheaper, better" development model which, he said, "pulled years of bark off
an aging procurement tree." He called on all of us in the space community to
be vigilant in the coming years as voices for "disarmament and demilitarizing
space would grow stronger and stronger, potentially denying us freedom of
action in space, and retarding the development of important technologies not
only designed to keep us safe, but necessary to continue to fuel the American
economic engine." As I sat that night, under the looming wings of the Spirit
of St. Louis, I couldn't help but be inspired by Schriever, his character, and his
accomplishments.

By the end of January I was hosting a constant stream of aerospace executives who came to talk about defense cuts, arms control, and space exploration…and the futures of their businesses. In one fashion or another they all
expressed the same concerns: pride and a strong sense of accomplishment with
the role their enterprises had played in waging and winning the Cold War on
the one hand and, on the other, worries, in the face of withering cuts in defense
research and development, about their employees and the rich technology base
they managed, as well as the choices they faced on behalf of the shareholders of
their businesses. And they wondered how the new space exploration initiative

would fare, how much they should invest in the effort, and whether we could win and sustain the support of Congress.

Probably the most memorable of these visits was that of Bill Anders, the new Vice Chairman of General Dynamics and anointed heir to then-CEO Stan Pace. Anders was a former Apollo astronaut, a member of the famous Borman-Lovell-Anders Apollo VIII mission, the first to go to the Moon and return, responsible for having taken the iconic "Earthrise" photo. Anders was a Naval Academy graduate and an Air Force pilot who had an enormously successful "second career" in industry – and he was my predecessor as Executive Secretary of the National Aeronautics and Space Council in the administration of Richard Nixon.

Anders came by to introduce himself late on a Monday afternoon in late January. He and I talked about the Council and how it had changed from his time in the office. He told me that he could immediately tell that we were more integrated into White House operations than he had been when he realized that our offices were in the Old Executive Office Building. He had been in the New Executive Office Building up 17th Street several blocks away from the White House. Anders told me that Vice President Agnew, who was Chairman of the Space Council, was completely disinterested in the Council, had spent more time playing billiards than working, and that Agnew spent most of his time in office laying low while waiting for indictments to fall on his tax evasion charges in Maryland. He said that OMB director Cap Weinberger had been something of a space enthusiast and so he was able to accomplish a few things, but, in general, the Nixon team viewed space as something for the "true believers" and something they hoped to cut after Apollo. In his final days in the White House Nixon's Chief of Staff, Bob Haldeman, called him into his office and told him, "Fire the President's science advisor, Ed David...and then pack your bags yourself."

After a brief discussion of the current Space Council operations, we then turned to the challenges Anders faced at GD. He was worried about the commercial space business and, in particular, the launch business. I told him that we were in the midst of a broad policy review of the commercial space business, especially space launch, and my view was that the administration was favorably disposed to doing all in its power to encourage and support commercial space and commercial space launch. But it was a complex matter involving fair trade and technology transfer as well as the whole issue of government subsidies for targeted industries. The fact is, we were already in the process of finalizing a Presidential Directive on commercial space that would lay out a broad range of policy initiatives designed to help commercial space grow and protect the business they already had, but which avoided the issue of direct operational subsidies for commercial space capabilities. Instead, the Directive emphasized the appropriate dual use of infrastructure funded by DoD and the civil space enterprise.

I asked Anders about defense spending and he explained that he really didn't know what to tell his shareholders and board members about the right direction for GD. Some of his shareholders viewed investments in GD as a patriotic duty in the past and saw lingering stock prices as a "necessary evil" of maintaining a private defense industry. He didn't know if the new circumstance and the resulting clear pressure on financial performance would sustain that sentiment. His view was that a massive contraction in the defense industrial base was on the horizon. The question for GD was whether they should compete to be the last man standing piled high with the debt necessary to buy and absorb their competitors or whether they should allow themselves to be sold in pieces to those who were in it for the long run, thus raising the greatest near-term value for their shareholders. Ironically, at that very moment, the Crown family of Chicago, who had been GD's largest shareholder since 1959, was making the decision to harvest the value in GD and provide a handsome return on the investment that they had foregone for decades. Within several years, Anders and his leadership team shed some of the worst performing elements of GD – and some of its most treasured jewels as well. In time, many of those in industry took to referring to the past-giant as "Residual Dynamics", ultimately composed "of the parts of the old GD that couldn't be sold." As Anders later observed, "When this is over, there will be one gorilla, two chimpanzees, and six marmosets."[31]

VII.

"TALENT IS GOD GIVEN. BE HUMBLE. FAME IS MAN-GIVEN. BE GRATEFUL. CONCEIT IS SELF-GIVEN. BE CAREFUL."

John Wooden

Relations with NASA continued to strain. DoD, DoE, and the National Academy of Sciences all reacted negatively to the 90-day study and the outreach program we asked them to sponsor to look for new ideas for conducting human space exploration. Carving out explicit roles for DoD and DoE in the initiative, as the President had now formally directed, was another blow to the NASA ego. The fact that the President himself and his White House staff continued to spend time and attention on space didn't seem to matter, and the fact that he backed up his words with deeds, requesting the largest increase in the NASA budget since Apollo (a whopping 24% increase year over year) seemed insignificant compared with the implied slight. This really perplexed and troubled the Vice President since he believed that the space exploration initiative was a significant statement of priority and represented a significant shift in the nation's R&D focus...all to the benefit of NASA. Hunkering down and protecting the status quo and defending turf over substance was exactly the wrong thing to do. And we were ever mindful of the loss of time and momentum with a Democrat-controlled Congress not eager to hand George Bush policy and programming victories, especially when they might come at the expense of the carefully apportioned jobs program NASA had become. That's why in February the Vice President requested a visit to NASA headquarters to meet and get to know the NASA leadership team and talk directly to them about what was riding on their performance in meeting the challenge the President had set for the nation. And he wanted the industry leadership team there as well so that there would be no distance between NASA and it's contractors in understanding what the Bush administration wanted and expected.

It was a cold and drizzly Monday afternoon on February 12 as the Vice President and I left the West Wing through the lower entrance. We drove to NASA headquarters in a full motorcade. NASA headquarters was right around the corner from the Air and Space Museum on the National mall and the drive couldn't have taken more than five minutes. There is something absolutely unearthly about travelling with the President or Vice President in a motorcade. The vehicle itself is quite conventional, although the windows are distinctly thicker, but the sheer weight of the significance of the convoy, the immediate attention and reverence it commands from everyone in its path is extraordinary. I found it difficult to converse while onboard. And while onlookers waved toward my side of the car, I had a constant urge to roll down the window (which, of course, is impossible) and say to the onlookers, "Relax – it's just me. The Vice President is on the other side!" Upon our arrival a crowd had gathered and Admiral Truly and his deputy, J.R. Thompson, stood stiffly at the curb, ready to receive their distinguished guest.

We went directly to the seventh floor, where the senior leadership of NASA was assembled to meet and greet the Vice President. He worked the room and stopped from time to time to chat with a member of the team. As he made his way around the room you could sense the growing relief and relaxation. Quayle, after all, is an outstanding politician and a genuinely nice person. Even hard-boiled bureaucrats, who probably were more than willing to accept the caricature of him that had been created, quickly softened to his personal charm. It never ceased to amaze me how much of an effect he had on people when they encountered him in the flesh.

Truly introduced the Vice President and explained that we would take a few minutes so the NASA managers could talk a little about the Agency and their role in it. Quayle listened intently and asked serious and thoughtful questions about space science, climate change, issues with the Shuttle, and challenges in the Space Station design. Quayle then spoke of the President's objectives for space and NASA, and said that NASA was a great agency with outstanding and dedicated people who had suffered too long without long-term direction and support from the White House. NASA was at its best when executing a mission that enjoyed broad national support and that was exactly what the President recently called for. Quayle talked about the need to keep technology flowing from the federal R&D enterprises, especially now and how DoD and DoE had brought incredible talent and resources to the table. We needed to utilize every resource available to us in a boundary-less fashion, he reminded them, in order to expand new horizons that could lead to whole new industries, new sources of energy, even new resources to make life on Earth better and more fulfilling. When he was finished, he thanked them for their support and efforts.

"The time," he said, "is for leaning forward, not leaning back; for looking forward, not looking back."

It was the first time a President or Vice President had ever visited NASA headquarters, and Dan Quayle didn't waste the opportunity.

At the end of the town hall meeting with NASA leadership, the Vice President, Admiral Truly, JR Thompson and I retired to Admiral Truly's office for a private meeting before we met with the aerospace industry executives. Truly thanked the Vice President for coming and for talking to the leadership team, and for his candor on the matter of Defense and Energy participation in the space exploration initiative. He said that he had been having trouble with explaining their participation himself. He thought the OMB language in the Presidential directive was disappointing and that it would fuel the perception that the Space Council and NASA weren't getting along. He explained that he hated the perception and felt that it hurt everybody involved. And then, astonishingly, he said, "The pounding that you personally have taken in the press is unfortunate and I would hate to think that more conflict, perceived or otherwise, could add fuel to that fire."

"Mr. Vice President," J.R. pounced, "the question is: is NASA in charge of coordinating this effort or is the Space Council?"

Quayle paused, then calmly, clearly, without hesitation, and with steel seriousness said, "You two have to knock this paranoia off. The Space Council is elevating the overall space program and working through the Council is having a major impact in the White House. There are many things inside this White House that the Vice President can do, things that affect DoD and DoE and that NASA could never do on its own. The fact is, the Space Council is and will continue to coordinate space policy, just as the President has asked us to. This isn't going to change and you need to get behind it and support it. The fact is the National Space Council is the best thing that ever happened to NASA. You have gotten more press and more exposure in the past nine months than over the last five years combined. Let's face facts: NASA used to be given a nominal amount of money each year from OMB and then left alone to fend for itself. This year, the President has requested a 24% increase in NASA funding and OMB protects it on the Hill as a Presidential priority. Do you think it is in NASA's interests, in the nation's interests, to go back? Do *you* actually want to go back to the old days? Well, do you?"

Truly and Thompson sat in stunned silence, shaking their heads, "no", like two students in the principal's office. The moment lingered for what seemed like an eternity.

"Now let's go see the industry team and see if we can't build a fire under them to get with the program." He put his arm around Truly like he would a colleague on the Hill, and walked him to the door – noting, in an offhand manner as they passed the threshold, "Nice office."

The session with the industry executives was smooth and, like the earlier meeting with the senior NASA leadership, Quayle was polished and persuasive. He knew almost all of the executives by their first names and joked with them about the weather and the outlook for defense spending coming from Congress. He spoke again about the President's vision, about the program we were embarking upon, and how much we needed their talent and ingenuity. He put his arm around Dick Truly again and said how much confidence he had in the administrator and explained that he had asked NASA to get behind what the President was trying to do.

He said, "It's a new day, and the space exploration initiative will be a multi-agency effort requiring unprecedented cooperation and focus on the government side – and I expect no less from the industry team." He took a few questions, largely about the level of support for space exploration on the Hill and about the "peace dividend," and then we were gone.

———

A couple of months later, the President did his part by hosting the first Congressional space summit in the White House in fifteen years. Senator Jake Garn from Utah, himself a former astronaut, had consistently asked me to call for such a White House summit to shore up support for the President's programs and budget request. We had tried to schedule the meeting twice, first in March and then in April, and it was finally on the schedule for the first of May.

The Vice President and I went to the Oval Office at 9:30am Tuesday morning May 1st, to prepare the President for the 10:00am meeting in the Cabinet room. We were joined by Dick Darman. The President was, as always, gracious and welcoming. He read that morning that the Hubble Telescope, in orbit for less than a week, was experiencing problems that threatened its usefulness. We talked briefly about the onboard antenna problem and the cord that was impeding the antenna's full range of motion, and therefore its ability to downlink data to Earth. The President said it was a shame and hard luck for NASA, but that he was also concerned that they were in the midst of a string of problems. He asked was there something "fundamentally wrong" within the Agency? Little did we know that the problems for the Hubble were just beginning and that its current communication problem would seem insignificant compared with those that would follow. Dick Darman suggested that we bring a model of the Hubble to the meeting in case we got into a discussion of the problem. We talked Dick out of this, as we had only an hour and did not want to risk chewing it up on something that no one in the room could contribute to in the least.

I left the President and Vice President a few minutes early and walked down the hall to the Cabinet room, already filling with members of Congress who were chatting in a fashion reminiscent of my earlier days on the Hill. I saw Jake Garn and immediately welcomed him "to the meeting *you* called." Jake was beside himself. He was grateful for our efforts and pledged to do all in his power to see that the President got what he wanted from Congress. Camera crews were massing at the threshold and we began to settle down when Dave Demerest stuck his head in and said, "The President will be here in a minute." We took our seats around the, famous Cabinet table and I noted that the back of each chair bore the name and department of the sitting cabinet member. It is customary that, upon departure from cabinet office, the cabinet chair bearing the official's name is given to him or her as a memento.

The door opened and John Sununu led the President and Vice President into the room. We all stood and Marlin Fitzwater, who had been holding the camera crews at bay, released a cord that had held them back. They immediately filled the room with boom lights and microphones. The casually attired crews stood in contrast to the suits and ties of the politicians around the table. It was like being on a movie set. Correspondents shouted questions about the release of American hostages from Lebanon that had occurred the day before and whether we were negotiating with the Iranians for their release. The President smiled and said, "I'm not going to rise to that bait; we are here to talk about space today."

The President led off with a short, focused discussion of his vision for the space program and how our civil space program needed clarity because it had been simply drifting for too long. He said the Vice President and the Space Council were doing a terrific job in helping him set and implement new goals for the country. We needed to focus on the Earth and its resources through the "Mission to Planet Earth", we needed to expand beyond the boundaries of our home planet with a new mission to the Moon and then on to Mars, and we needed to define and complete the Space Station so that we could learn to work and live in space for long periods before venturing to new worlds. President Bush said this was not only "in the American character," but that it was important to start thinking about the world after the Cold War and how we would advance our technology and keep our economy growing once we had achieved the peace for which we had worked so long. He then turned the floor over to the Vice President, who talked about the Council and our activities. The Vice President explained that we were moving to meet the President's challenges, seeking the best ideas and new technologies to accomplish our goals faster and cheaper, without sacrificing safety, all while building the new infrastructure and new technology needed to keep the United States in a leadership position, not only in space, but in the global economy. The President thanked the Vice President and then turned it over to the members.

We had anticipated that comments would start from the leadership, but Bill Green, a House Republican from New York and the ranking member of the House Appropriations Committee for HUD, VA, and independent agencies (which included NASA), and anything but an advocate for the space program, spoke first.

Green launched into what amounted to a tirade against the manned space program. He said that Mission to Planet Earth and the Earth Observing Satellites were the only projects worthy of support from Congress. He claimed that the American scientific community was unanimous in its condemnation of human space flight and the wastefulness of the entire manned space program. He concluded by saying that funds for science and technology were better focused on the National Science Foundation and the EPA than NASA.

The President looked shocked. No one had prepared him for this attack. He turned, almost with a small degree of desperation, to Speaker of the House Tom Foley, who immediately came to the rescue. Foley distanced himself, with respect, from Congressman Green and told the President that he and the majority of Congress were strongly supportive of the space program and agreed that we urgently needed to look to, and invest in, the future. He said that the House was going to work on a substantial increase for space and that, while they may have had disagreements about exactly what our future in space would be, they were in strong agreement on the need to provide funds for it. The President then said, "Well look, let's stay with the House side." He went to Dick Gephardt, who made a very strong pitch on this being "exactly the kind of thing America ought to be investing in."

"It has a great impact on children and students," he added, "and provides inspiration for millions of Americans of all generations." It was a strong statement.

The President then turned to Newt Gingrich and said, as he pointed to Newt, "Let's just stick with the House."

Newt Gingrich gave a very strong vote of support for the program, the need to fund it even as we struggled with the deficit, and the need to look to new technologies and the private sector for carrying some of the load.

Then the President turned to Senator Allen Cranston from California, sitting in for Majority Leader George Mitchell. Cranston had a reputation as being somewhat "cool" on NASA and space, but he said, quite surprisingly, that this was a very important program for the State of California and so he had a parochial interest in the matter. Beyond that, he added, speaking for Senator Mitchell, the initiative enjoyed great support among the Senate leadership and they would be happy to do anything they could to support the program. Senator Bob Dole, Republican Leader, then gave a good, strong statement of support for the program and cautioned the President against relying too much on a "peace dividend", which, he said, "may well be less than we hope for...the fact is, the world remains a very dangerous place."

Senator Howell Heflin of Alabama, known among his colleagues as "The Judge" because of his service on the Alabama Supreme Court and his outsized Faulknerian appearance, sought recognition and talked about the need for creating a space trust fund and the problem of the appropriation process being spread between HUD, VA, and independent agencies. He turned to Barbara Mikulski and she reiterated what Heflin had said, observing how difficult the choices were. There was some light banter about smoke and mirrors in last year's appropriations bill, and she twisted Dick Darman's tail a bit by saying that when it came to his "cherished field of space," he was willing to accept all manner of budgetary shenanigans to get what he wanted. She expressed her support for the program but told the President how tough it was going to be inside the 302B budget allocation (the budget resolution document that determined just how much money the HUD, VA, and independent agency appropriations bill would have to spend among these activities).

The President then turned to Senator Garn – who modestly quipped that he wasn't going to say anything because they had all been subjected to Jake Garn speeches on space for so long that he wanted to spare them. But he did observe the institutional problem posed to Congress of having the appropriations – originally a grab bag of HUD and independent agencies – now pitting EPA against NASA, and EPA and NASA against Housing and Veterans. The appropriations process, he said, would have to be reformed, or some independent permanent source of funding for space would have to be found before we could really shift into higher gear.

Bill Green then interjected again, railing on one more time against the manned space program. Quayle wouldn't let this line of reasoning go unchallenged. He questioned Green's assertion of consensus in the scientific community and talked about his personal meetings with members of National Academy Sciences Space Studies Board and their support for manned space as part of a balanced program – precisely the kind of program, in fact, that the President was offering. He said that Green was entitled to his own opinion, but that he should not hijack the opinion of the National Academy.

The President then said, "As you can see, the Vice President is fully engaged on this matter." He turned to Senator Jack Danforth – the tall courtly Republican from Missouri, heir to the Ralston Purina fortune, and an ordained Episcopal minister – and asked him to close out the meeting. Danforth is a calm and careful legislator with a soothing style and a gentle demeanor that made him a perennial favorite among his colleagues. Danforth summarized the meeting and then said that we really needed to look at our aerospace industry, what the future might hold for it, and how much trouble it was going to be in as a consequence of reductions in defense spending and the end of the Cold War. He said that the American economic miracle of the late twentieth century had strong roots in the advanced technology developed for our nation's security, much of it coming from our aerospace industry. He said that while we celebrated the peace that may come from the end of the Cold War, we could not turn our backs on the critical role our national technology program played in our economic success.

"We all in this room," said Danforth, "are responsible for America's economic future now, and what the President has done and what he is asking us to do today is important and wise and deserves our support."

The President thanked everyone, got up, and left the room. The remaining participants lingered in the Cabinet room for a few minutes and I told Senator Garn that I hoped he wasn't going to depart without meeting with the waiting press since it was most likely that Congressman Green was going to share his thoughts with them. Garn said that he would be happy to go out and tell them what an uplifting and important meeting it was.

VIII.

SO CLOSE, YET SO FAR

"Ah, but a man's reach should exceed his grasp, / Or what's a heaven for?"
Robert Browning

By late spring 1990 difficulties for Mikhail Gorbachev and the Soviet Union were mounting. Unrest in the Baltics had crystallized in Lithuania with a standoff between local Lithuanian leaders and Moscow, resulting in an enforced blockade by Soviet forces stationed there. This, in turn, put pressure on the United States to interject itself publically into Warsaw Pact politics, which, in turn, intensified Soviet resistance to American "interference." All the while, domestic economic pressures were eating away at Gorbachev's freedom of action on glasnost and perestroika. What had been anticipated as a spring of rapprochement and progress in US-Soviet relations was turning into a tense confrontation on the issues of German reunification and participation in NATO, trade, and the Baltics. As President Bush recalls, Gorbachev "was presiding over a rotten economy; the probable election of Yeltsin, his bitter enemy as President of the Russian Federation; and struggle over the Baltics and other nationality problems."[32] Leaders of the Communist Party and the military were expressing their displeasure with Gorbachev's perceived weakness on Germany and Lithuania and his inability to deliver on the economy. Reformers, like Yeltsin, were criticizing Gorbachev for going too slow and accommodating the Party over the welfare of the people.

I continued to work with NSC and State on proposals and potential agreements with the Soviets on space, but signals were mounting that the ministerial meeting between the Secretary of State Baker and the Soviet Foreign Minister Shevardnadze in May and summit between Presidents to follow in June were likely to be difficult and the atmosphere was probably not right to discuss new cooperative initiatives in space exploration. Nevertheless we prepared for the Summit. What Gorbachev needed most was trade relief and evidence that he could stand up to American pressure in the Soviet sphere of influence – and cash, especially cash. What the Bush administration needed was a stand down of the Soviet blockade of Lithuania, a nod to reunification of Germany and the accession of Germany in NATO, and movement on conventional arms control in Europe. In mid-May, it was difficult to see how the pieces could all fit together and how a train wreck could be avoided.

At the same time, conditions in the US economy were starting to show signs of weakness. High interest rates, declining corporate earnings, and a looming crisis in cleaning up the Savings and Loan debacle were all pressing on a deficit that was tipping towards $160 billion. President Bush faced a budget deadlock and the prospect of automatic, draconian budget cuts mandated by the Gramm, Rudman, and Hollings Budget Act. A restive Congress called on the President for tax increases and more rapid cuts in defense. Secretary of Defense Dick Cheney tried to hold the line while bowing to new geopolitical realities in the world. On June 18, Secretary Cheney held a press conference to announce administration plans to reduce US defense forces by 25% over a five-year period and cut defense spending by 10% over the same period. While this came as a welcome sign to House and Senate Democrats – a sign that the administration was beginning to soften on its stance on national security – it was far from their expectations for cuts in spending. The day after Cheney's press conference, *The New York Times* reported that "Representative Les Aspin, the Wisconsin Democrat who chairs the House Armed Services Committee, called the plan 'one of the seminal events in this year's budget debates....[H]owever we are no where in terms of the budget number. Instead of cutting military spending ten percent, I favor something in the mid twenties.'"[33]

The White House was caught in a vice grip between Congress and the Soviets in what appeared to be a zero sum game.

Planning for the June summit had begun very early. I received a letter from Secretary Baker in mid-March asking for a series of issue papers and specific recommendations for space cooperation proposals for discussion and potential tabling at the Summit. By early May this had become an agenda item at the highest levels. But on May 10, the Vice President attended a Summit-planning meeting with the President and Brent Scowcroft and reported the President had said, "Given the current status of US-Soviet relations, it looks like the summit is going to be pretty business-like and a little on the clenched jaw side; we might not be signing new agreements on space cooperation." He said, however, that he liked the ideas the Vice President had offered and was especially interested in our Shuttle-Mir idea. By the 13th of May, only a day before the Summit advance team was to leave for Moscow, Condi Rice stopped by my office and told me, "It's now pretty clear that the Summit is going to be pretty grim." The Soviets were apparently backing away from agreements on Germany and Lithuania; there was a growing sense that both the ministerial and summit would be short.

When Condi returned a week and a half later, she reported, "The Soviets are a little better than they were in April, but are, generally speaking, still pretty bad actors." They had completely gone in the tank on Germany.

"We're back to square one," she said. Apparently the Russians had been shocked and stung by the actions of the "four plus two" meeting that had taken place in Bonn on the 5th of May. The "four plus two" group was made up of the original four powers of WWII that held joint custody over Berlin and supervised post-war Germany: France, Britain, the United States, and Russia; the "two" were West and East Germany. The United States had proposed the "four plus two" meeting a means of addressing and disposing of the German reunification matter. In Bonn, the western three had stood squarely for reunification without condition, leaving the Soviets outnumbered, outmaneuvered, and now, apparently, out of sorts.

Two days later, however, on May 25th, Reggie Bartholomew from State called and said things were improving and perhaps space initiatives *would* make it onto the Summit agenda. He asked that we "revalidate and update" our specific proposals, which we did immediately.

By Tuesday the 29th we were in final preparations for the Vice President's one-on-one meeting with Gorbachev, scheduled for Friday June 2 at 2:00pm. It was mid-afternoon when I got the call from Cynthia to join a meeting in progress in the Vice President's ceremonial office in the Old Executive Office Building. When I arrived, I found the Vice President, Bill Kristol, John Glassman, and Carnes Lord pouring over the Summit briefing papers as well as notes from the ministerial and subsequent staff conversations. They told me they were proposing that Quayle use his time with Gorbachev to express his views on central matters, ranging from trade to Lithuania and Germany, but he would not mention START (Strategic Arms Reductions Talks) and CFE (Conventional Forces in Europe). They then turned to me and asked, "Should he mention space?"

"Should he mention anything *else* should be the question," I replied. "Look, the best that could possibly be accomplished by the VP during the meeting with Gorbachev would be confirmation of what Gorbachev already knows and is already in the process of negotiating. The worst is that somehow Gorbachev detects (or invents) a deviation, however slight, in the VP's position. This could cause a whole set of problems for the Summit and possibly even leaks from detractors in the administration that 'Quayle screwed up'. Why on earth would we want that? I suggest that the Vice President use all of his time to talk about space – something no one else, it now seems, is going to do, and that he be prepared to respond to Gorbachev's questions if he wants to probe a bit. Who knows, we could initiate a whole new line of discussion and potential agreement in the Summit."

Quayle looked up and instantly agreed, "Yup, that's it. Let's talk about space and nothing but space. I'll talk to the President and Brent, and let's take Kristol and Glassman and Albrecht to the embassy meeting."

With that he was off to the West Wing, where the President was about to convene his "small group" on Summit preparations. When he returned two hours later he called and said, "The President was in complete agreement. I will focus on space, but be completely prepared to respond to other topics if Gorbachev is looking for another avenue on a topic already under discussion."

On June 1, 1990 newly elected President of the Russian Federation Mikhail Gorbachev arrived in Washington for a summit meeting with the Bush administration. It was time to lay cards on the table, but as the Gorbachevs' motorcade arrived that Wednesday morning at the White House South Lawn, space cooperation and our lead proposal for a Shuttle-Mir astronaut and cosmonaut exchange were still in the summit notebooks.

On that hot Thursday morning, President Gorbachev and his wife were driven around to the South Lawn, where President and Mrs. Bush were waiting to greet them. The entire senior staff was assembled in a semi-circle around the driveway. Flags and Colonial-style honor guards festooned the entire area. We applauded when the doors opened. The Presidents greeted one another, reviewed the spectacular array of troops, and walked together into the Diplomatic Reception Room. The White House staff left the South Lawn and returned to our offices, where the balance of the day was a mix between frantic dashes between the OEOB and the West Wing, with motorcades racing off in various directions, and the routine business of White House operations. I, for example, had scheduled a late lunch in the White House mess with Admiral Truly and his deputy, J.R. Thompson, and was anticipating the standard Thursday mess special, and personal favorite – Mexican food – when the Mess Captain came over to our table, as we were sitting down, and said, "Condi Rice is looking for you and needs to talk to you immediately."

I went to the small room just outside the mess entrance, where a phone was waiting, A breathless Condoleezza Rice was on the line, "I understand that the State Department is planning on signing an agreement on space cooperation with the Soviets at 3:00pm today and they tell me it has all been approved by the Vice President. Is this true? Do you know anything about it?"

I didn't. I immediately called Reggie Bartholomew to find out what was going on. Reggie was in negotiations with the chief Soviet arms control negotiator, Viktor Karpov, a veteran of US-Soviet talks since 1969. Reggie's deputy took the call and said that yes, they planned to go ahead with the Shuttle-Mir proposal, that they had a sign-off with Baker the night before, and that Reggie had understood his conversation with me on Friday constituted a West Wing sign-off on the issue as well.

I immediately tried to contact the Vice President, but he was with the President and Gorbachev in the Oval Office at that moment. I called the Space Council's office to get a copy of what it was that State was proposing to table with the Soviets; to my surprise, the language had been delivered to us earlier in the day, although there had been no indication that it was going to be tabled.

I tried to call Condi Rice but couldn't get through to her, so I quickly escorted J.R. and Dick Truly out of the White House mess and went upstairs to see the VP, who had just come out of the meeting with the President and had escorted Gorbachev to his car. He told me that he was totally unaware of this development. We went down the hall to see Brent Scowcroft and found Scowcroft and Baker discussing the Oval Office meeting between the President and Gorbachev, at which Scowcroft had been note-taker. The Vice President walked in and said to Baker, "Hey, I understand you are going to sign a space agreement at 3 o'clock today."

Baker said, "No, I don't know anything about it." The Secretary of State held out a sheet with the items under discussion and their current status; there was a line at the end of each that said either "closed" or "open", and after that a place for notation on whether the item would be contained in the master agreement or side agreement.

"It looks pretty thin," Baker commented, "The agreements look pretty thin. Maybe we should add it? What do you think?"

Quayle said, "Well, I don't know. It is a reasonable thing to do. The real issue is, have you talked to the Soviets about it and are they interested?"

Scowcroft didn't say anything, and finally Baker said, "Well okay, we will add it to the list."

As we came out Brent's office, I started to think, "Well, maybe this might be an interesting idea." We went upstairs and talked to John Bowright at the State Department and told him what had happened and he said, "Should we take this as an indication that it is now on the agenda?"

Since Scowcroft hadn't said anything at the time I said, "I don't think we should characterize the views of the NSC. You ought to get those directly." Will Toby from the NSC then called and said he would try to clarify with Scowcroft what his understanding was regarding the outcome of our meeting. All the while we were preparing "backgrounders" for the press and the sudden possibility of signing a space agreement.

I finally got in touch with Reggie, who was caught off guard. He said Baker had signed off on it the night before, but since he himself had taken a break from the negotiations with Karpov he didn't know where things now stood. It was almost seven in the evening and time was not on our side.

Will Toby called me again with word that Arnie Cantor had talked to Scowcroft and that Scowcroft felt that the matter was a bit more inconclusive than Baker had suggested. Scowcroft said that, in any event, he was going to turn the issue over to Condi Rice.

I then called Condi, who said, "Well, it hasn't been tabled with the Soviets yet, so we haven't really introduced it. It is awfully late in the Summit. Do you think we really ought to do this?"

I agreed that it was late – the State dinner scheduled for that evening was looming – and we didn't want to upset the apple cart without preparation on the Soviet side. That induced a call to Baker's Policy Planning Chief, Dennis Ross. Dennis claimed that Baker was misinformed when he had said that it had already been discussed and presented to the Soviets; it had not, and so Dennis's view was that it was too late to bring up in the Summit. In any event, Dennis added, an astronaut-cosmonaut exchange would be a very high visibility element of the Summit, one of the perhaps two or three most significant agreements outside of arms control and trade. It would certainly be one of the only positive outcomes and one that might send a mixed or even wrong signal of where we stood. All these arguments were precisely why we had decided the previous week that it might not be a good idea to include it in the Summit agenda.

Reluctantly, I agreed that we had simply run out of time. Tomorrow was going to be devoted largely to meetings on the Hill and some ceremonial visits around town by the Soviet President. The Vice President had almost an hour scheduled with Gorbachev at the Soviet ambassador's residence in the afternoon, but that certainly wouldn't be the time to table as complex a proposal as an astronaut and cosmonaut exchange. And the President had put out the word that the time at Camp David on Friday night and Saturday would be for informal talks only – no negotiations.

The Vice President's meeting with President Gorbachev the next afternoon at the Soviet ambassador's residence was interesting, but ultimately anticlimactic. We arrived by motorcade just before 2:00pm. A crowd of the curious had formed at the awning extending from the front door to the curb and across the circular driveway that opened to busy 16th Street in northwest Washington. The residence was built by the Pullman family of railway fame in 1910 and sold shortly thereafter to the Russian government; it had been used as the official state embassy until 1983, when a massive new complex, strategically placed on the heights of Washington DC – at the nexus of crucial microwave relay towers – was officially opened as the Soviet Embassy. The Pullman mansion remained the ambassador's residence, however, and was a beautiful artifact of turn-of-the-century Washington, serving as the downtown social headquarters of the Soviet mission.

We entered the mansion and proceeded to the main reception area on the second floor. A large crystal chandelier hung in the open atrium; a large formal circular staircase led upstairs. Through the hallway under the staircase we could see a formal dining room with large glass doors covered with sheer linen drapes. To the immediate left of the staircase was a sitting room, or small parlor, painted in Romanov red, with two gilt chairs and a coffee table on the intricate parka floors in the center, facing a mirrored wall. Cameras had been strategically placed at the entrance of the parlor and crews from the media pool mingled somewhat awkwardly with Soviet security staff, Secret Service, embassy staff, and the small party of the Vice President, his Chief of Staff, myself and security advisor John Glassman. It was an odd mix.

Within a moment or two, the Soviet President appeared at the top of the staircase and descended to the hallway to greet the Vice President. Quayle then introduced each of us to the President in an impromptu receiving line. Gorbachev was business-like in demeanor, working his way from Kristol to Glassman to me, giving us each a firm handshake and short nod before moving on to the next. He then took the Vice President by the arm and motioned for them to enter the parlor and take a seat. Cameras rolled as the two leaders each said a few words in English about "progress at the Summit" and "things going well". An interpreter entered the room with the leaders, the doors shut behind them, and we waited in the hallway.

About halfway through the meeting, Prime Minster Edward Shevardnadze emerged at the top of the staircase. He was highly agitated, talking loudly to an aide, who accompanied him down the stairs. Something was clearly wrong. When he got to the bottom, he noticed our entourage standing in the hallway.

Looking awkward and somewhat surprised, he nodded and looked about for another place to wait for the President. As he went, he continued to engage in an animated discussion with his staff, his voice continuing to rise for the better part of five minutes. Later, on our drive back to the White House, we were to learn the cause of his anger. Final preparations on the joint communiqué had hit a bump on the matter of Most Favored Nation trade status. This was one of President Gorbachev's most highly coveted prizes of the Summit – one which he needed badly. President Bush had *privately* agreed to a compromise on Lithuania that would allow the President to withhold submitting to Congress approval of MFN trade status for the Soviet Union until the Soviet blockade of Lithuania ended, but would not announce the fact that he was doing so. In short, the public announcement at the summit would be that the United States was moving ahead on MFN status, however a side and non-public agreement would stipulate that this status would not be requested of Congress until the blockade ended. Apparently one draft of the public communiqué missed this nuance and the linkage explicitly appeared in a version of the document shared with the Soviets for public dissemination. This was a potential disaster for Gorbachev because it would imply to his hardliners that sovereignty was being exchanged for agreements on trade.

At the appointed time, Quayle and Gorbachev emerged from the parlor, embraced, and parted the Vice President and our group down the staircase, Gorbachev and his to the urgently waiting Shevardnadze. As we moved to the waiting White House motorcade, the Vice President shook a few hands on the rope line that had formed across the street, as many onlookers cheered and waved upon his appearance. As he worked the line, Quayle noticed Coretta Scott King, who, with several others, was speaking with the Soviet security team awaiting their meeting with the Soviet President. He walked over and greeted her warmly. They spoke with for several minutes. He then turned, entered the limo and we sped off to the White House.

According to the Vice President, Gorbachev had asked for Quayle's help on the Hill regarding the trade matter and, in turn, expressed enthusiasm for space cooperation. "Let's go to Mars together," he had offered. Quayle said that Gorbachev was a serious man, clearly under pressure to deliver at the Summit and facing strong headwinds within his own country. He seemed tired, said

Quayle, a bit distracted and overwhelmed with the schedule to which he had agreed. Among topics the two discussed were Cuba and Soviet support for the Castro regime. Gorbachev wryly observed, "Castro has taken to criticizing *me* lately." Quayle responded, "Well, we are used to being criticized by Castro; it isn't that bad. Nevertheless, we don't give him seven billion dollars of annual support." The CIA had supplied the figure to the VP. Gorbachev quickly corrected, "It is five billion a year. No more."

Once again, though, cooperation on human exploration between the Soviet Union and the United States had eluded our grasp. We believed that involving the Russians in establishing solid medical baselines of the long-term effects of space on humans might be an additional stimulant for NASA in thinking about the design and function of the Space Station, and it might provide an opening for new thinking about the entire space exploration program. Clearly the Soviet space program needed a boost – in prestige, in commitment, and most of all, in cash. The mutual benefits of this cooperation were high, despite the inability of both sides to surmount the larger geopolitical issues in the spring of 1990. After the Summit, Condi, Reggie, and I agreed that we would continue to press the issue; we agreed that Baker would table it at the October ministerial with Shevardnadze and that we should aim for late winter to complete the agreement, capped by a trip to Moscow in the spring of 1991 to kick it off. Little did we know that events around the world and inside Russia would effectively pull this plan off the table for over a year. It would take that long for the opportunity to again come to the surface, but that time we wouldn't miss.

IX.

NOT IN OUR STARS

The fault, dear Brutus, is not in our stars,
But in ourselves, that we are underlings.
Shakespeare, *Julius Caesar*

The spring of 1990 wilted into a sweltering Washington summer. Troubles were mounting for the Bush administration's agenda, and our relations with Congress were fraying fast. Turning to the budget, the whole town was bent on extracting a piece of the post-Cold War "peace dividend." Most favored cuts closer to House Armed Services Committee chair Les Aspin's 25-percent than Defense Secretary Dick Cheney's preferred 10-percent.

Congress was also vectoring a large chunk of defense funds to new priorities that had little chance of spurring aerospace innovation. Sam Nunn, head of the Senate Armed Services Committee, was carving off a portion of the defense authorization for a new "environmental enterprise" within Defense. Nunn attached to his proposal a series of ongoing safe programs, like Landsat, the long-running acquisition of imagery of Earth from space. His rationale was that the environment was rising to the level of a national security threat and the Defense Department needed to treat it that way.

At the White House we shared Nunn's view that the Departments of Defense and Energy had enormous technical capabilities and that the country should focus on new problems. But we didn't see how his vague "environmental studies" could rival space exploration as a technical springboard for the twenty-first century. Further, unlike space exploration, Defense hadn't much interest in environmental studies.

But Nunn's machination paled next to the sudden surge in a new legislative slight-of-hand we were starting to see lawmakers use to fund pet projects: the earmark, whereby the lawmakers cryptically claim chunks of funds in the defense budget for non-defense projects, such as a museum, a useless airfield, or a community swimming pool to serve as a monument to the said member of Congress. In the early 1980s there were about fifty earmarks per budget. By 1990 the number topped 500. By the mid-1990s earmarks in defense bills routinely surpassed 1000.

Closer to home, President Bush's new Space Exploration Initiative (SEI) was under attack. One week Democratic House Speaker Tom Foley was stoutly defending the initiative at the White House; the next week he was zeroing out funds for it in the NASA appropriation bill. We watched our requested 24-percent increase get slashed in half. The appropriators wrote the NASA bill essentially from scratch—business as usual—and NASA rolled over.

Behind the scenes rumors circulated among our allies on the Hill that NASA was "tepid" on the president's space exploration idea and actively derided it as the "S.D.I.-ing of NASA," a reference to President Reagan's Strategic Defense Initiative (sometimes known as "Star Wars"). We ignored the rumors and pressed the administration's agenda as one team, the White House and NASA, until a June 29 *Washington Post* article hit: "House Stops Attempts to Trim $83.6B Spending Bill." In the first paragraph, reporter Dan Morgan noted, "The House also eliminated for the time being $300 million for the Moon-Mars initiative, a top priority for the President, but not NASA. Representative Robert Walker (R-PA) suggested in an interview that appropriations had been influenced by 'bureaucrats from NASA who come up here to say, the President thinks this is a good idea, but we don't think so.'"

Now we had an internecine war on our hands that we couldn't ignore.

The White House senior staff meeting that week wasn't pleasant. When "the NASA matter" came up, Chief of Staff John Sununu was furious.

"What the hell is wrong with NASA?" Sununu yelled. "Don't they know who they work for? Fix this right away. I don't want to hear about this again. Understood?"

For NASA, the timing could not have been worse. That day another shuttle developed a mysterious hydrogen leak and the agency was forced to stand down the entire shuttle fleet pending a top-to-bottom design review. The leaks had begun with Atlantis in May, then spread to Columbia in early June, and now Atlantis again.

The leaks were embarrassing but didn't compare to the day's next problem. A colossal quality escapement essentially rendered the multibillion-dollar Hubble Space Telescope useless, and it was already in orbit. It appeared that the optical lens of the telescope had a spherical aberration, created during fabrication, which caused the optics to focus on the wrong point in space. The effect was blurred images, useless for scientists to study back on Earth.

NASA's performance was raising staff blood pressure at the White House. Word began circulating that a high-level, external full review of the space program was in order. The President had gone out on a limb for NASA, against prevailing political wisdom that the public was fickle on space. Instead, the President had embraced it, supported it, and charged NASA with leading a new, expansive mission. Now perception was growing that the Agency was the gang that couldn't shoot straight.

To top it off, it appeared that the Agency was openly undermining the White House on the Hill. Several "frank and candid" exchanges ensued between the White House and NASA head Dick Truly. Even Vice President Quayle called Truly to make sure he got the picture. I called Lew Allen, director of the Jet Propulsion Laboratory at Caltech and retired Air Force Chief of Staff. NASA had just asked Allen to investigate the Hubble failure. I told him that the White House was interested in his new assignment and asked him to be thorough and frank. We were troubled by the Hubble and shuttle problems, I told him, and also by the lack of cooperation on the President's new proposal.

I encouraged Allen to take the broadest liberty with his charter so he didn't miss important insights, even if they didn't bear directly on Hubble. Allen was smart and thoughtful, a remarkably modest man considering his accomplishments. He told me that he would do his best and that he intended to use only Defense Department experts to safeguard the study's independence and integrity.

"Our first priority is root cause," Allen told me. "Our second is corrective actions but we won't spare observations about process and people if that needs attention."

The immediate NASA mess resolved itself thanks to OMB director Dick Darman's deft intervention on the Hill and some awkward press availabilities by Administrator Truly. But the damage inside the White House was done. We clearly needed a thorough, independent assessment of NASA, its organization, management, and program plans. Truly also needed to show that he was willing to listen and change the way the agency operated before we got back to work.

The G-7 Summit that the President was hosting in Houston that July was a perfect opportunity. Vice President Quayle asked me to round up a small group of independent-thinking space experts—advisors from the programs of manned space and space science, veterans of NASA management, and Defense Department officials with NASA experience. Quayle wanted knowledgeable people who were discreet and spoke plainly. He wanted a serious, no-holds-barred discussion about NASA and its future.

Houston in mid-July is hotter than a rodeo pistol. I flew down early to visit the Johnson Space Center to look at plans for a new mission control and talk to officials about the President's exploration initiative. That night, Gene Cernan hosted a small dinner at his suburban Houston home for the group from which Quayle would seek advice. Cernan, a former Navy pilot and astronaut was the last man to stand on the Moon, in 1972, and had become an author and businessman. A plainspoken man with an athletic build and shock of white hair, Cernan proudly retained his Chicago accent and tackled issues head-on. He was concerned about the Agency's mission drift, its balkanized center structure, and its overwhelming bureaucratic inertia.

Tom Paine, former NASA administrator and retired CEO of Northrop Corporation, also joined the group. Paine was a genial man with a spine of steel. He had the difficult duty of guiding NASA through the Apollo mission flight years, first as James Webb's deputy, then as administrator himself. He left NASA in 1970 when he failed to convince President Nixon that the U.S. should build upon Apollo and continue its long-term exploration agenda. He simply could not preside over the orderly and terminal completion of Apollo. Paine was a passionate advocate for space exploration and America's pioneering spirit. In 1985, he led a Presidential commission on defining America's future in space. He was more polished than Cernan, more bureaucratically astute, and troubled by the fecklessness of NASA's response to President Bush's Moon and Mars challenge.

Bruce Murray, former director of the Jet Propulsion Lab, was probably the most opinionated member of the group. Murray was an intense and somewhat impatient man with an improbable combination of trendy mutton sideburns and 1950s era hair that looked like so many pictures of 1970s fathers caught in a personal fashion struggle between old and new. He had a hard Clint Eastwood-like stare and a sharp mind.

The last member of the group was Hans Mark, a German-born, naturalized American citizen who had quickly navigated America's premier institutions of science and engineering. He was a graduate of the fabled Stuyvesant High School in New York City, star of UC Berkeley's undergraduate physics program, and leader in MIT's doctoral physics program. And he hadn't done too badly in his professional life either: Secretary of the U.S. Air Force, director of DARPA, deputy administrator at NASA. At 61, he was chancellor of the University of Texas and displayed all the signs of a guy who was just getting going.

Mark was openly critical of NASA. Tall and trim with short cropped grey hair, bushy eyebrows, his steely blue eyes flashed when he offered several specific organizational changes he thought were needed to right NASA's ship. Mark also probably had the most obvious conflict of interest: he wanted Dick Truly's job as administrator.

Our timing was good. As we sat down in Houston, NASA Deputy Administrator J.R. Thompson was sitting down with ABC's "Nightline" to discuss the contagious shuttle leaks, the catastrophic problems with Hubble, and whether NASA was capable of fixing itself. Cocktails in hand, we gathered around Cernan's television and watched Ted Koppel methodically destroy J.R.;

Tennessee Senator Al Gore, appearing later on "Nightline," also spared no criticism, although he chalked them up to NASA being "overextended" more than fundamentally flawed. Gore's comments didn't help our request to put more on NASA's plate.

The next day, the five of us joined the Vice President aboard Air Force Two for the flight from Houston to Washington. John Sununu and Craig Fuller, who had been Bush's Chief of Staff when Bush was Vice President, joined us. Fuller and Sununu sat across from the Vice President at the working table. Cernan, Mark, Murray, Paine and I perched on the arms of adjacent chairs while Quayle led the discussion. To set the stage, the Vice President asked me to review the administration's space exploration initiative and the series of technical and performance problems plaguing NASA.

Nobody held back. Paine said that the system itself was rotting NASA from the inside. Talented people were leaving the Agency, frustrated with the bureaucracy, he said, and the remaining staffers were primarily "bureaucrats and technocrats." The best and the brightest from the Apollo years were long gone.

Murray agreed. The only way to get new talent to flow back into the Agency was to convince management to embrace new ways and new thinking, and to clear dead wood from the upper reaches. Only then would contractors, tired of short leashes and job-shop direction, invest in and partner with government. Murray pointed to the Jet Propulsion Laboratory as a model to follow. JPL was lean and focused on the mission. It partnered with industry to innovate and squeeze every bit of value out of every appropriated penny.

"We have almost no bureaucracy," Murray said, "and everyone is consumed with getting the most, and the best, science out of the missions. NASA and industry operate as a team at JPL, with mutual respect and mutual account-ability."

Hans Mark pointed to the Agency's wasteful independent center structure. NASA is an enormous hub-and-spoke institution issuing commands from its Washington headquarters. But it executes most of its work through a tangle of large research centers dotted across the country. They launch in Cape Canaveral, Florida. They operate from Houston, Texas. They build in Huntsville, Alabama. They research in Cleveland, Ohio. They design and test in Hampton, Virginia.

Every NASA center had become a local high-tech jobs program with enormous political influence. The loose center structure made it virtually impossible for effective overall agency planning and execution. Without fundamentally addressing the paralyzing center problem, Mark said, NASA would drift over the edge and into oblivion.

Sununu took it all in, famously multitasking, signing and annotating all manner of documents and shuffling papers, while listening to the discussion. After an hour, Sununu raised his head.

"The real question is: is there a core at NASA that is worth saving?" he asked with characteristic dispassionate distance. "Not the top management, we can change that overnight. But we can't change the middle managers, the engineering and technical backbone. So I ask, is there a core at NASA that is worth saving or do we need to throw the whole Agency out and start over? We do not want to get into a situation where we are simply painting over a carcass."

He reiterated the statement he had made months ago in the Vice President's office. "Look," he said, "I went to graduate school on a NASA grant. But if we need to shut it down, we need to shut it down."

Tom Paine addressed the question squarely.

"I can't say for sure whether we have reached the point of no return yet," he said. "We may well have. But I think we need to give NASA one more chance, to give Dick Truly one more chance to face reality and do those things that are necessary to make sure that NASA doesn't die of its own weight."

Fuller observed that every administration has the opportunity to take a top-to-bottom look at major programs, organizations, and agencies. Surely the Bush administration would have the opportunity to do that with space. After all, the President had repeatedly said that civil space was critical to America's future. No one could attack him for trying to kill NASA.

Consensus quickly formed for a Presidential commission to review the civil space program. Everything from programs to plans to structure would be evaluated to determine whether NASA could meet the demands of the administration and Congress. Everything would be on the table, including the very existence of the Agency itself.

Quayle and Sununu said they would take the commission idea to the President right away. They were sure he would support it.

"We spoke about NASA in Kennebunkport three weeks ago," the Vice President said, "and the President told me he was concerned about the space program and asked that I consider actions to deal with mounting problems at NASA. This is a reasonable and necessary step. After this we will have all options available to us and a solid basis for action, if that is what is necessary. No one wants to hurt the institution, and no one wants to impugn the excellent people at NASA. But the country is heading into new waters and we need the technical vitality of our aerospace and high technology infrastructure to continue to move forward. We carved out a central role for NASA in all this and it's critical that they are capable of carrying the load. We simply can't get this wrong."

After landing at Andrews Air Force Base, I rode with the Vice President in his motorcade to Capitol Hill for his meetings with the Senate leadership on pending appropriations bills. I called Dick Truly from the car as we drove and asked him to meet me in Quayle's ceremonial office just off the Senate floor to discuss the newly hatched NASA commission plan. The limousine pulled up to the covered lower entrance to the Senate and the sergeant-at-arms greeted us.

For me, the Senate was familiar turf and the halls never failed to bring back fond memories and chance encounters with old friends and colleagues with whom I chatted about politics and Senate business. Like much of the Capitol, the Vice President's ceremonial office is decorated in an ornate neoclassical style that always reminds me of the country's robber baron past. Small medallion portraits grace the walls, likenesses of Daniel Webster and John Calhoun among them.

I met Truly in a small office just off the Vice President's suite. Truly was nervous but friendly and I got right to the point.

"As you know we have been concerned about technical problems with NASA," I said, "and quite frankly with the way you have handled the President's space exploration initiative." I told him I realized we had discussed it many times before but now the President and Vice President wanted to take some bold steps to assist him in hitting some important goals. "We're forming a commission to look at NASA top to bottom—programs, plans, performance, organization, the whole nine yards."

Truly looked stunned.

"Mark, I don't see how this helps at all," he said. "It's only going to pour gas on the situation. The only problem NASA has is some technical issues with the Hubble and shuttle hydrogen plumbing. Those will be fixed and we will be on our way. Anything that draws further attention to NASA, especially Presidential attention, will only make the job harder."

Truly was defensive and his argument was more plaintive than persuasive.

"I hear you Dick," I said. "But you must understand that the President has invested an enormous amount in NASA and he's beginning to take serious heat about your performance. And your opposing his wishes on the Space Exploration Initiative up here on the Hill has caused his team to ask, 'What are we doing?' We need to rebuild confidence in NASA and frankly you have lost the ability to manage that task from inside. Your credibility has been compromised."

A call came in requesting that I join the Vice President in the Majority Leader's office for an appropriations meeting. Truly begged me to reconsider. Then he asked a personal favor: If the commission was a done deal, have it report to NASA so the Agency could save a little face. I told him I'd consider it.

In Washington, the outside world has a way of taking control of things you were pretty sure you controlled. Two days after my meeting with Truly, Paul Gigot of *The Wall Street Journal* wrote a column about NASA and the "flight from Houston." He reported about a midair "caucus of space nonconformists" advising Vice President Quayle aboard Air Force Two about "the need for new thinking." Gigot winked, "The last person to talk like that was Mikhail Gorbachev" – whose Soviet satellite nations had been declaring independence all spring. Gigot went on to describe the problem confronting the most pro-space administration since Jack Kennedy's: "It can now decide to defend NASA, hoping that the next fiasco occurs on somebody else's watch. Or it can lead an effort to shake up or kill the plodding behemoth that NASA has become."

The *coup de grace* came swiftly but no less painfully: "Space exploration is a worthy government enterprise, in principle," wrote Gigot, on his way to becoming journalism's most influential voice of free markets, "especially for a nation that has long defined itself by the frontier. But arthritic bureaucracies don't tame new frontiers. NASA is even losing to those ultimate bureaucrats, the Soviets. Just as housing is too important to leave to HUD, space is too important to leave to NASA."

Ouch.

The weekend brought major television network stories alleging that the Bush administration was weighing the fate of NASA Administrator Truly and whether to disband NASA altogether. CBS News's Leslie Stahl went so far as to speculate that NASA would be terminated in a week. The media overreach, typical though it was, caused an immediate halt for plans to announce of a Presidential commission on NASA that week and added further impetus to Truly's plea that NASA direct any commission.

Two weeks later, after the dust had settled and the attention of the media had moved on, the White House rolled out the Presidential commission to review the civil space program, under the leadership of Norm Augustine, CEO of Martin Marietta and former undersecretary of the Army. While the White House wrote the charter, and selected the chairman, and all the members of the commission (with input from NASA), I granted Truly's request and made sure the commission was a NASA commission that would report to NASA and was answerable to NASA leadership. But Augustine also understood that while the commission nominally "reported" to NASA, its primary customer was the White House and its focus was nothing less than "a complete assessment of NASA."

What began as a small indulgence of Truly's sensitivities turned into the second major mistake I made in my Council leadership. There was the "routine" certification of the Space Station that I had recommended for the President's approval a year earlier. Now, letting NASA take ownership of what would become known as the Augustine Commission, ultimately delayed by a fateful margin of months the changes that NASA simply had to make in order to create an opportunity for them to rise again.

Change ultimately did come to NASA – just not in time. That July we could not have known that we were only days away from Iraq invading Kuwait and the start of the first Gulf War. Our efforts would be placed on hold for more than a year, and then they would be thrust into a hotly contested Presidential election and finally, into the hands of a Democrat-controlled House and Senate.

X.

"THIS WILL NOT STAND."

President George H.W. Bush

On August 2, 1990, after a series of threats, ludicrous claims of sovereignty, and saber rattling on the border, Saddam Hussein's Iraq invaded neighboring Kuwait under the pretense of a coup and the installation of "new leadership."

No accounting of the events of August 1990 could improve on the exhaustive reports of President Bush and Brent Scowcroft in *A World Transformed*. As the President recounts, on August 1 his "mind that evening was on things other than Iraq. We were in the midst of a recession and an ugly, partisan budget battle. Strained meetings with the congressional leadership were underway to find a compromise. There were other pressing foreign troubles catching my attention as well, such as hostage-taking in Trinidad and a tragic civil war in Liberia, in which Americans were in danger."[34] Within hours, the focus of the administration would be on Kuwait. Within days, the focus of the entire national security apparatus of the United States would be on the Middle East. As Brent Scowcroft was to observe several days later on a flight to Aspen, Colorado, where the President would be "setting forth a new military strategy and force structure in response to a winding down of the Cold War": "it became obvious to me that the President was prepared to use force to evict Saddam from Kuwait."[35]

Six months later we were at war, leading an unprecedented international coalition of forces to compel the withdrawal of Iraqi troops from Kuwait and to restore legitimate Kuwaiti authority. In doing so, the United States would field the largest combined-arms military force since the Vietnam War, at its peak comprising over 500,000 soldiers, sailors, marines, and airmen. Marshalling world attention on Kuwait, leading the UN Security Council to pass a series of resolutions condemning and sanctioning Iraq, assembling a 33-nation coalition to enforce those UN sanctions and forming a coalition military command structure to lead those forces, informing and preparing the American public and consulting with Congress leading to a successful vote on support for military action, and eventually prosecuting near flawless military operations in the Gulf – all this necessarily consumed the White House and the administration from August 1990 until the summer of 1991. And rightfully so.

Needless to say, the President's space exploration initiative, the creation of a new "federal space enterprise," the transformation of NASA, and the conclusion of new agreements with the Soviet Union for serious space cooperation aimed at streamlining US manned space efforts saving time and money were all necessarily, and quite appropriately, removed from front-burner Presidential priorities.

By September, 1990, there were 200,000 American troops in Saudi Arabia, ready to repel any attack on the Saudis by Iraqi forces. The Pentagon was beginning to work with Congress on massive supplemental bills to pay for those operations, supplemental bills that would eventually exceed $50 billion by the Spring of 1991. A figure that was almost twenty percent of the entire Defense appropriations bill approved for FY91. Aerospace companies, DARPA contractors, research institutions, and suppliers across the Defense industrial base worked day and night to support the effort and the Pentagon asked for all the capability the system could produce. As one executive said to me in the fall of 1990, "Saddam Hussein may have single handedly saved the American aerospace industry." This sentiment may have been more wishful thinking than prudent planning, but events in the Gulf did have the effect of temporarily easing the economy's post- Cold War "traumatic stress syndrome". The Joint Chiefs of Staff – who only weeks earlier had implored us, because of their "unique perspective relating to space technology and the space exploration initiative," to include JCS representatives on Space Council Interagency Working Groups on issues like international cooperation – found it more and more difficult to attend Space Council Working Groups at any level. And Congressional appropriators who were already struggling with 302B budget allocations for the HUD/VA and IA appropriations account, which included NASA, had strong new reasons for restraint when it came to "new initiatives" like space exploration.

Nevertheless, and with the active encouragement of what limited attention we could garner from the White House, we pressed ahead with our work through the balance of 1990 and the first half of 1991. The Augustine Commission performed admirably in the fall of 1990, issuing an exhaustive report in December, less than thirty days before the launch of Operation Desert Storm. Like the constituent members of the Commission, the report itself was careful, measured, and politically sensitive. And it was balanced. No one was immune from criticism, including the administration, which was described as "overburdening" NASA with mission requirements without forging a national consensus beforehand on what the mission should be. Since the Commissioners seemed to support all ongoing activities from aeronautics to educational outreach, everyone read and used the report for his or her own purposes. The Space Station and the Shuttle were singled out for restructure and reduction, but neither was marked for cancellation. We needed new launch capability, new engines, new technology development, more space science, a mission focus on planet Earth, a long-term manned exploration on a "pay as you go" basis, and a steady increase in resources amounting to 10% per annum.

NASA management was hit the hardest. The commission described poor program management, poor project performance, poor systems engineering, and poor communications with the White House and Congress on all of the above. While the Commission spared the axe that we simply start over with civil space, a careful reading of the lengthy report must conclude that the Augustine Commission report was a major indictment of NASA. For example, the Commission commented on recent technical escapements at NASA and observed that NASA required, "redundant, flexible designs, explicit test procedures, independent checks and balances, unwavering discipline and, above all, inquisitive, penetrating, and challenging people – people who are not satisfied merely to fill the squares of regulations but rather are continually questioning and ferreting out anomalies to be placed in full view of all involved." The clear implication was that these were capabilities the Agency had in short or nonexistent supply.

Incredibly, but perhaps not surprisingly, NASA largely ignored the Augustine Commission report. As Dick Truly had said to me back in July, as he implored me to abandon the idea of a Commission altogether, "We will fix the leaks, correct the Hubble, and get on with the program." Other than public praise and appreciation for a "job well done" and some subsequent changes to the faces and spaces at NASA headquarters, there was little changed as a significant consequence of that report. Neither the Space Station nor the Shuttle program were fundamentally redirected or reduced, there was no appreciable change to the space science program, no significant new technology developments were undertaken, and the long-term space exploration program remained orphaned inside NASA, as it had been all along. Within a year, it became obvious that without change at the top, NASA was on a course that could not, would not, be altered.

When the White House finally concluded that a change in leadership was the only course of action, I recalled a telephone call that I received from Bruce Murray shortly after our "flight from Houston" in July 1990. Murray had said that he believed Tom Paine had a specific purpose in his recommendation that "Dick Truly be given a chance to make changes at NASA based on recommendations from the outside." He had said Tom was certain that Dick would not be capable of making significant change at NASA and that therefore, would be replaced. Tom had been right.

Perhaps the most important and largely unnoticed legacy of the Augustine Commission is that it marked the end of America's "First Space Age." We had reached an inflection point by 1990: the space race with the Soviet Union had been won, our preeminent position in space for the time being was assured, yet we could not define compelling new horizons, new motivations were lacking, the core program was wearing thin with the public, and agency performance on what remained was flagging. While we had worked to move NASA and the nation's space enterprise to the next level — a sustained and ever expanding engine of technology advancement, economic achievement, and global leadership without a Cold War as engine — the Augustine Commission provided a respectable and responsible blueprint for sustaining "the flat part of the curve":

an excellent, if not routine, civil space science and technology thrust of the federal government that would set its sights based on our wallets not our will, and that would reflect the nation's values, not its aspirations. It was, and remains today, the recipe for comfortable, bureaucratic middle age.

Without a doubt, plans for an American renaissance in space exploration to pivot, not pause, at the end of the Cold War were bogging down. But our strategy included another element: cooperation with the Russians. It was a plan to share costs, field "best of breed technologies," and harness the vast Soviet R&D enterprise for peaceful purposes in a new and dangerous world where would-be regional bosses – like Saddam Hussein – were all too eager to offer a life-line to Russian technologists, engineers, and scientists in exchange for dangerous technology. In 1990 we crafted and approved a plan for starting the engagement with a Shuttle-Mir astronaut exchange, but had not been able to find the right opportunity to close the deal. Desert Storm put all that on hold while we focused on the stability of the "world transformed." But behind the scenes, the entrepreneurial drive and imagination of our aerospace industry strategized on ways to utilize and profit from cheap, advanced Soviet space technology for commercial, if not governmental, purposes. As usual, the free market didn't need consensus to move; opportunity is defined, risk assessed, and action taken. Plans for a joint Russian-American space enterprise were taking shape, even while the government attended to other matters.

PART III

I

"THEY WILL BEAT THEIR SWORDS INTO PLOWSHARES AND THEIR SPEARS INTO PRUNING HOOKS.

Nation will not take up sword against nation, nor will they train for war anymore."
Isaiah 2:4 & Micah 4:3

I left the White House in the summer of 1992 having been a federal employee for almost ten years (Senate and White House time combed) and facing the daunting financial prospect of paying for three college educations. In truth I was tired. After almost four years of turbulent relations with NASA, the unprecedented and forced removal of an administrator, and the hiring of a new NASA leader, who I had high hopes would reset relations with the White House and take charge of a much needed top-to-bottom restructure of the Agency and its programs, it was simply time to go. Although friends subsequently have admired my apparent "shrewd insight" in leaving the Bush White House months before the improbable election of a little known Arkansas

Governor – largely as a consequence of the vain, quixotic, and quirky candidacy of H. Ross Perot – I fully anticipated a successful reelection campaign for the 41st President.

Within weeks of my departure, President Bush and President Boris Yeltsin met in Washington for their first formal summit where an entire package of space cooperation initiatives was finalized. It included a new element: a request by the Russians for the United States to support the use of their workhorse launch vehicle, the Proton, for two commercial missions, first the launch of an Inmarsat telecommunications satellite and second the launch of a cluster of small spacecraft that would become part of the Iridium mobile phone project. The agreement was signed in June 1992 and the Russian commercial space business was born.

Yet even while I was packing my office for departure senior leaders of many major aerospace enterprises were actively preparing for the impact of a looming "peace dividend" decline in defense spending on their business portfolio, market position, and future.

In 1992 the Lockheed Corporation of Calabasas, California, with a Space Systems Division in Sunnyvale, was staring at a financial abyss unlike anything it had seen since 1971, when Congress famously "bailed out" the aerospace giant to ensure development of the L-1011 aircraft, competitor to the Boeing 747 and the McDonnell Douglas DC-10. Lockheed was currently looking at a potential 50% reduction in revenues, which would necessitate severe employment cuts.[36] There were several holes in the Lockheed portfolio since the demise of its commercial aircraft business, but none were as gaping as in space launch and the potential for participating in the lucrative and growing commercial space launch market. General Dynamics had the Atlas rocket, McDonnell Douglas had the Delta rocket, and Martin Marietta had the Titan rocket, all converted ICBM's fully capable of launching commercial payloads from government launch sites at Vandenberg in California and Cape Canaveral in Florida. While Lockheed owned the US franchise for submarine-launched ballistic missiles, those missiles had no practical capability for carrying government or commercial satellites into orbit since they had no land based launch infrastructure, hence the company had few prospects for the new space commerce. Lockheed was looking for a bridge to a "new aerospace economy." They were open to opportunity, led by Dan Tellep, a visionary artist and engineer committed to keeping the company afloat and intact. At a board meeting in August 1992 CEO Dan Tellep was prodded by board member led by Dean of Stanford's Engineering school, Jim Gibbons, to consider what Lockheed might do with the newly "liberated" Russian aerospace industry. Despite Tellep's career as a Cold War engineer who helped develop the nuclear warheads for sea-launched ballistic missiles aimed at the Soviet Union, he didn't flinch.

Within a month, Lockheed managers were working with Stanford faculty member Bill Perry, a former senior defense official in the Carter administration and later Bill Clinton's defense secretary, to develop a plan to engage Khrunichev Space and Research Center in Moscow in a partnership for the commercialization of the workhorse of Soviet space launch, the legendary Proton. With the approval at the Bush-Yeltsin summit, Khrunichev already had two commercial customers. The innovative business plan was crafted by a Missourian, Mel Brashears. Mel was a young PhD from Mizzo and had a fast rise at Lockheed. He exuded a certain mid-western frankness and confidence that bordered on arrogance. These characteristics contributed both to Mel's significant success as well as his ultimate undoing at Lockheed. Brashears reasoned that Lockheed's experience, access, and expertise in satellite manufacture and space operations would complement perfectly the Proton's enormous lift capacity in order to offer commercial customers high quality, high confidence contracts, payload processing, and launch operations, all under the watchful eye and responsibility of one of America's most respected and important defense and aerospace contractors. Brashears' plan was for a joint venture between Lockheed and Khrunichev, with Lockheed providing the seed capital to start the business and Khrinichev providing the Proton vehicles and launch infrastructure. The equity would be equal, but the proceeds from individual contracts would be split on a fixed, pre-negotiated schedule of revenue sharing. Each partner would manage its own part of the business and earnings would accrue based on the cost structure of each partner. As a consequence there would be no "earnings" at the enterprise level and no distribution on an equity share basis. This structure would minimize governance and ownership issues and keep each partner at arms length on internal cost and accounting practices. It was a creative, if not ingenious, scheme, but it would be a complex deal and Brashear's reasoned that negotiations would probably take months or even a year.

To the surprise of all, Perry suggested a trip to Moscow immediately and so Brashears rushed to complete the concept and proposal, ran it by his boss, the former Deputy Director of the CIA, John McMahon and then finally, Chairman Dan Tellep. But Lockheed approval was only the first step. Something as novel as collaboration between two of the world's most secretive repositories of national security technology could not happen spontaneously. This would require at a minimum the attention of the White House, if not its approval. So Brashears not only had to gain the approval of the National Security Council and my old organization, the National Space Council, as well as the State Department, the CIA and Lockheed's chief customer, the Department of Defense. All in two weeks.

The Bush administration was quick to recognize the opportunities of such an arrangement and with uncharacteristic speed gave Mel and Lockheed the "OK" to enter discussions with Khrunichev. By the end of October, Brashears and Perry and a small team comprised of Aspen Institute consultants, with whom Perry was then associated, and Lockheed specialists arrived in Moscow for meetings with Anatoly Kiselev and the Khrinichev management team.

Brashears recalled the visit as a combination tourist trip, undercover reconnaissance mission, and routine business deal negotiation.[37]

The Russians were enthusiastic to meet with the Lockheed delegation and were eager to show the team everything in their once-super secret space technology production center. The tour of Khrunichev Space and Research Center, including its newly acquired Design Bureau, KB Saylut, lasted almost three hours. Launch vehicles under construction in a massive production line, Mir space station modules and components, test equipment, production facilities — all were open to the American team. Brashears and his group were mightily impressed by the size and scope of the operation, the advanced technology, the efficiency of the production line, and the almost surreal sight of what "a day without OSHA" might look like. Without harnesses, workmen scrambled over enormous pieces of equipment, tiny catwalks without rails towered over the plant as engineers crawled like ants along the cavernous superstructure. Brashears asked his host, "Do you have accidents? Have you lost workers?"

Kiselev smiled and replied simply, "Workers must be careful; nevertheless, we have replacements." The presence of cats roaming among the delicate machinery seemed somehow eminently practical once explained: "Mice can get into small pieces of hardware."

After the plant tour, the party retired to a small conference room at the heart of Khrunichev. The Americans sat on one side of the table and Anatoly Kiselev and the Russians on the other.[38]

Mel Brashears began the meeting by thanking Anatoly and his team for the remarkable tour of KhSC and proceeded to describe the Lockheed proposal to Anatoly Kiselev as if Anatoly were another American executive. Because he was not, he was unaware of US corporate financial and legal terminology. Mel was not getting across, and Anatoly was not getting the story as a coherent message.

Although enjoying the complimentary references to Proton, Anatoly began to appear visibly edgy and frustrated, as were the other Russian participants. The one-sided conversation reached its climax when Mel introduced the subject of ownership split, explaining that Lockheed, as the principal investor in the joint venture, was entitled to a majority stake and would have at least 51%.

Anatoly's face reddened. "So you are saying," he interjected, "that our Proton is a great booster and you want it to be the centerpiece of the proposed joint venture." As he spoke he was taking off his jacket. That done, he asked: "Is this my jacket?"

Mel, visibly bewildered, said, "Yes, yes!"

"And you want half, in fact more than a half, of *my jacket*?"

He then proceeded to almost tear it apart.

The interpreter, Valery, swore he heard the sound of fabric being ripped. He stepped forward. Valery explained to Mr. Brashears that he and Mr. Kiselev were not on the same page. Anatoly was under the completely false impression that Lockheed was proposing to "absorb" Khrunichev's Proton production business into Lockheed. He interpreted Mel's 51% formulation as a complete buyout, with a share of future commercial revenue as Khrunichev's sole compensation.

Once he understood the true nature of a "joint venture" and the sharing of commercial revenues, Anatoly smiled and said: "Aha! Well, now, that's a different story!"

The conversation continued peacefully for a while, to everyone's relief. However the conversation again became tense when Anatoly suggested that, in addition to the agreed investment of $15 million into the joint venture, Lockheed should provide a separate amount of $5 million before the year was out in order to finance "Proton modernization", as Kiselev put it.

Suffice to say, the Lockheed team's reaction was mixed.

"We have no authority to agree or disagree beyond that first amount," they answered. To which Kiselev responded by saying that telephones were available both at Khrunichev and at the hotel, or at the US Embassy, and there was a lot of time left in the business day (which had not even begun in the US) to call Lockheed headquarters and get appropriate answers. He said it was the condition for any deal. If Lockheed should vacillate, "we will have Boeing here within minutes." It was one of Kiselev's first bluffs — although Boeing *was* rumored to be on the prowl.

The parties then agreed to meet the next day with the answer to the five million dollar question. They discussed a few additional points of agreement which they would put on paper and sign as the minutes of the meeting.

When all arrived at Anatoly Kiselev's office the next day, he was pleased to hear that the matter of additional funds was resolved. Within a week, the entire team was to reconvene in Sunnyvale at the Lockheed facility and there the final agreement was reached and signed. LKEI, or Lockheed, Khrunicvhev, Energia International was immediately formed.

Within three months of the contract signing, on January 1, 1993, the Russian military-industrial complex ground to a halt. Funding was no longer coming from the federal budget. Thousands of employees had their wages delayed by many months — but not at Khrunichev. As agreed, on December 30, 1992, Khrunichev received $5 million from Lockheed. Khrunichev never missed a payment to its employees. In a few months, regular progress payments started coming in from Lockheed as consideration for Khrunichev's services. The first commercial joint venture between American and Russian aerospace industries had been birthed.

Eight years later, I would be running the successful venture as Lockheed Martin's President of International Launch Services.

II

THE "NEW" RUSSIA

During the night I inadvertently left open the smallest seam of the shade on the large oval window at my shoulder. As I rolled over in my bed to face the window, with the persistent high pitched hum of the jet engines clearly audible through my earplugs, I could see the faint edge of light in the distance. I reached over and eased the lever down, drawing the interior shade of the Gulfstream window open wide. There before me, against an almost perfectly black sky, was the reflection of moonlight on the vast, white terrain of the flat, seemingly empty Russian plain below, ever so dimly lit by the suggestion of dawn still more than an hour away. It was November 28, 2000 and I was onboard the Lockheed Martin corporate Gulfstream heading to Moscow to meet with our business partners from Khrunichev Space and Research Center, senior Russian officials, and with our customer, Sirius satellite radio. The launch of the third and final satellite of the new constellation would provide almost one hundred channels of CD-quality music from space anywhere in the continental United States.

In three days we would launch the over-twenty thousand pound Sirius 3 satellite from Baikonur Cosmodrome in Kazakhstan, a secret Cold War space facility deep in the Eurasian land mass we called Tyuratam during the Cold War. The launch was scheduled for launch in the middle of the night onboard the massive Proton launch vehicle, which would send it into a highly elliptical orbit known as a Molnyia orbit, first utilized by the Russians in the late 1960s for their early warning satellites. The name, "Molnyia" derived from the

Russian word for "lightning," due to the enormous speed a satellite in this orbit achieves each time it dips low towards the Earth's surface in its perigee orbit. Once around the perigee, the Molynia satellite is lofted almost one-tenth the distance to the Moon, there to slowly dwell over the apogee portion of the orbit. Sirius 3 was to join Sirius 1 and 2 in a synchronized set of such orbits that would provide full and continuous coverage of the entire continental United States. As one satellite set into the perigee portion of its orbit, another would rise through its long duration apogee. As a result, two satellites remain in perfect view from anywhere in the US at all times – perfect for broadcast, as our customer had concluded, and for surveillance, as the Russians had earlier found.

Eight years earlier, in 1992, I left the White House, and in 1999 I was named President of Lockheed Martin's International Launch Services (ILS), a partnership between the new defense giant Lockheed Martin and the premier launch vehicle manufacturer of Russia, Khrunichev. The formation of ILS was a consequence of the Lockheed and Martin Marietta merger in 1995. Martin had purchased the storied Atlas launch product line from General Dynamics in 1992 and offered a commercial version, the Atlas Commercial Launch Service (ACLS) to complement the services they already provided the US government. Since 1993, Lockheed was marketing the Proton rocket launch service through it's partnership with Khrunichev Space and Research Center and Russian Space Corporation Energia under the name, Lockheed Khrunichev Energia International (LKEI). By joining the two enterprises, the newly formed Lockheed Martin Corporation created International Launch Services (ILS), bringing the Atlas and the Proton to the commercial market and the Atlas to the US government.

By the mid 1990s, as we had predicted, the US defense industry had undergone the most extensive contraction since the end of World War II. In 1992 there had been over sixteen prime contractors capable of manufacturing and supporting major combatant weapons systems for the Department of Defense. By 1998, there were three. Russia had long since abandoned Soviet-style Communism, as well as its empire, and was in the throes of defining "democracy in the new Russia." By 2000 catastrophic economic chaos accompanied the flight of billions of dollars of capital from Russia and a crushing devaluation of the ruble started in 1998. The Russian economy was in shambles and the International Launch Service business, which had grown from the collaborative space efforts started in the Bush administration and aggressively pursued in the Clinton administration, had become a significant source of hard currency inputs for the Russian economy. Our productive engagement of tens of thousands of Russian aerospace engineers and manufacturers intimately knowledgeable with ballistic missile technology provided added incentive for the United States government to encourage and support this relationship. Ironically, we had become at once the *agents* of the US government, in helping to control ballistic missile technology proliferation and providing desperately needed hard currency for the Russian economy, and *hostages* of the same US government for the billions of dollars of business we had at risk with the Department of Defense and NASA should a breach of technology security by our Russian partners ever occur. It was, to put it mildly, an interesting time.

I was traveling to Moscow that day with Al Smith, Executive Vice President of Lockheed Martin for Space Systems. Al presided over the $7 billion space enterprise at Lockheed Martin. The Space Systems division included the former Sunnyvale Lockheed plant in California, which specialized in the manufacture of classified and unclassified satellites and submarine-launched ballistic missiles, and the former Martin Marietta plant in Denver that boasted its own satellite work as well as manufacture of the behemoth Titan IV launch vehicle and the Atlas launch vehicle. Smith's portfolio at Lockheed Martin also included the International Launch Services business venture with the Russians which he had overseen seven years earlier at Lockheed before the merger. Al grew up on the south side of Boston in a large, working-class Irish Catholic household. Al is smart and ambitious. He left the south side of Boston to attend Northeastern University, where he studied engineering working nights to pay his tuition. Al joined the CIA as a young engineer right out of college to see the world. While Al escaped life in working class south Boston, he retained local tastes in food and drink and entertainment, and a love of street-smart politics. He had a lot in common with Mel Brashears, his predecessor at Lockheed Martin. But unlike Mel, who was an introverted engineer who kept his modest Missouri roots under cover, Al was an extrovert and relished his modest roots. Al was a star at Lockheed and later at Lockheed Martin, and had become a first class aerospace manager who looked every bit the part of an accomplished executive. At heart, Al was a Boston "Southie," a man of simple tastes. He worked and played hard and never forgot where he came from. He was a perfect fit for our Russian partners. They liked and respected Al and he felt the same way towards them.

As our Gulfstream descended across the outskirts of Moscow in the dawn, we could see buildings through the thin layer of clouds that was beginning to yield a light snow on the small farms and villages along the narrow roads below. Soon the roads gave way to larger, grey concrete complexes, and the distinctively orange fluorescent lights over highways of the city, leading toward Sheremetyevo International Airport sixteen miles northeast of Moscow.

In our large overcoats, gloves and hats in hand, we made our final approach to the airport, anticipating the blast of arctic air we knew would accompany the opening of the cabin door once we came to a stop on the tarmac. We had been to Moscow many times in the winter and were under no illusion about the conditions: it would be cold and snowing. As we touched down and rolled down the runway, we could see the littered remains of the scavenged carcasses of abandoned Russian aircraft – used for spare parts or simply long-term corrosive storage. It was like a well-lit scrap heap. We wheeled to the sequestered part of the facility where corporate jets parked, and passed the massive concrete terminal building, a traditional, soulless Stalinist facade capped by an enormous and instantly recognizable carved laurel wreath encasing the hammer and sickle flanked by large wings. Every time I arrived I always felt like I was entering the movie set of a post-apocalyptic film.

That early morning ride in the dark limo to Moscow was as familiar as it was depressing. Rows and rows of beautiful birch trees on snow-covered, gently rolling hills, with distinctive bark that reminded me of American Indian canoes, quickly gave way to grey repetitive blocks of apartment buildings. These in turn merged into neon-encrusted stores and restaurants and massive and repetitive billboards offering all manner of household products and luxury items and, of course, cigarettes. These cheery and modern billboards always seemed out of place in stark contrast with the grim conditions on the ground. Moscow traffic was always horrible, with cars and public transportation buses in generally decrepit condition and large trucks belching exhaust darting dangerously

in and out of traffic. There were always numerous vehicles abandoned at the
side of the road — inoperable, the victim of an accident, or simply run off the
road by aggressive commuters. Everyone was smoking, and as we approached
the city and the morning hustle and bustle grew amid the snow and slush on
the streets and sidewalks, we could clearly see the Muscovites bundled in hats,
scarves, boots, and galoshes waiting for public transport.

We eventually turned into the awning-covered entrance of the Kempinski
Balchug Hotel in downtown Moscow. After a brief and expedited registration
I went to the 6th floor room I had had many times before. As I entered the
suite, I was immediately drawn to the large bay window in the center of the
sitting room. There before me were the still-illuminated great brick walls of
the Kremlin and the famous Spaaskaya Tower with the giant red star atop its
steeple. Below Spaaskaya spread Red Square, with St. Basil's Cathedral at the
center. The Kempinski Hotel was directly across the Moskova river from Red
Square and adjacent to the Bolshoy Moskvoretsky Bridge originally built in
the 15th century as a wooden bridge over the most narrow part of the river. In
the 1930s, Joseph Stalin had initiated a modernization effort within Moscow
that included replacement of all major wooden bridges with modern concrete
ones. The old Moskvoretsky was replaced by the Bolshoy Moskvorestsky in
1938. The view of St. Basil's was stunning. The cathedral, with its whimsi-
cal ice cream-cone cupolas and brightly colored geometrical patterns edged in
gold, had been built by Tsar Ivan the Terrible in 1561 to celebrate his victory
over the Tartar Mongols in 1551. Legend has it that Ivan was so struck by
the beauty of the finished product that he had the architect Postnik Yakovlev
blinded to ensure that nothing in Russia could be designed to rival its beauty.

As the morning spread across Moscow, I retreated for some sleep before we
started what I knew would be a very long day.

III

"Toto, I've a feeling we're not in Kansas anymore..."

Dorothy, *Wizard of OZ*

We departed the Kempinski in the early afternoon and made our way through the bustling Moscow streets towards the Khrunichev Space and Research Center on the outskirts of the city. As in many European capitals, driving in Moscow is an adventure – the streets are crowded, the drivers fast and aggressive. Our driver was expert in the ways of Moscow traffic, but his intense focus and tight grip on the wheel signaled that even he respected the danger that was all about. The city is ringed by bridges and beltways and large boulevard arteries that radiate from the center towards the outer limits. On our way to the Khrunichev plant we passed Poklonnaya Hill and the large monument that marks the spot where, in September 1812, Napoleon's Grande Armée established a final encampment before entering Moscow for what Napoleon was certain would be surrender by Tsar Alexander I. Not only did Alexander refuse to surrender, General Turkev abandoned the city and within hours it was set ablaze by the Russians themselves as the ultimate act of denial and defiance. From this spot, Napoleon proceeded no further, and by early October his long march back to France – and final defeat – began. What had started in early June as a campaign with close to one-half million men marching to Moscow, returned that December, bowed and bloodied, as a rag tag militia of fewer than 20,000. This is regarded by the Russian people as the greatest victory in the "Patriotic War", and was an important symbol of their grim determination and nationalistic spirit. The grand overture of Tchaikovsky's 1812 symphony is the spiritual hymn of Russian nationalism and a reminder of the suffering and sacrifice that characterizes all of Russian history. Napoleon made a mistake of hubris that was be repeated one hundred and thirty years later, in the "Great Patriotic War" by Hitler at Stalingrad.

The Khrunichev facility provides a glimpse as to its place in Soviets life during the Cold War and the secret Soviet society of space and missile technology. The outer boundary of Khrunichev is ringed with large grey walls. There are no signs, no logos, no indication of what lies within, and only a single narrow road carved in the snow approaches the compound. Passing through multiple heavily guarded checkpoints, we entered the main compound, which was instantly recognizable to our team as a large manufacturing and fabrication facility. Large cryogenic tanks were attached to high bay assembly plants. The adjacent railroad cars and rail tracks clearly indicated how steel and aluminum, and component pieces such as crated engines from Energomash arrived, and how the finished product, the mighty Proton launch vehicle, left after completion. In order to avoid American surveillance these "rocket trains" usually left under cover of darkness, on the long journey through the Steppes of Russia to the high desert plains of Kazakhstan.

As our cars wound their way through the narrow factory streets in the light snow, we noted very few workers at the facility. The setting sun through the grey skies and light snow cast an eerie light and lent the place a dark and foreboding mood. Despite the fact we had made this journey many times before, we always felt we were entering the past world of Soviet Russia for the first time.

The cars finally stopped in front of a grey, fluorescent-lit square concrete building, the headquarters of Khrunichev Space and Research Center. Several black BMWs were parked in a random pattern in the snow near the front. Large men in black leather jackets loitered in front of the building, in or near the cars and on the steps to the front entrance to the building. Almost all of them were smoking.

We were hurried from the cars, through the slush on the road and into the building. The inside was a complete contrast to the manicured defense plants we were accustomed to in the United States boots, not dress shoes, were the order of the day when visiting Moscow. There we were, senior executives of Lockheed Martin Corporation, the largest defense contractor in the world, stamping snow and slush off our dress shoes at the entrance to a bunker of a building that looked more like an emergency relocation facility or inner city school than an aerospace headquarters.

As we climbed the plain concrete stairs lit by long fluorescent bulbs, a chilling breeze filled the empty hallways and bare concrete walls. The place reeked of anonymity and plainness. We came to a recessed double door and entered the main Khrunichev conference room. The conference room, in contrast to the rest of the building, was warm, well lit, well appointed, and modern, with wood paneled walls and a large wooden conference table and comfortable leather chairs. The walls were decorated with jumbo photos not unlike those I knew from the White House. These depicted US and Russian dignitaries and Khrunichev executives touring the Khrunichev plant facilities. Vice President Al Gore, Boris Yeltsin, Vladimir Putin, NASA administrator Dan Goldin and his Russian counterpart Yuri Koptiev. All the photos included the likeness of the Director General of Khrunichev, Anatoly Kiselev.

As soon as we were seated and had greeted our Khrunichev colleagues with warm bear hugs and back slaps, the doors of the conference room opened and in walked Anatoly Kiselev. Kiselev was sixty-two years old, itself a rather significant feat given the fact that the average lifespan of a Russian man was just over fifty years. He is a large man with large appetites. He flashed a broad, crooked smile and showed childlike excitement at the sight of the Lockheed Martin team. One by one, Kiselev embraced each of the team members and made his way to the empty seat at the large conference table.

Kiselev is a complex man. Unlike most of his contemporaries in the Soviet era aerospace industry who had attended the best technical universities in Russia, were close to or even members of the Communist Central Party, and who started in management at the elite Design Bureaus, Kiselev had been a shop

steward in the Khrunichev General Machine Building plant in his early twen-
ties, having earned a certificate from a trade school. While working on the plant
floor, Kiselev studied for advanced degrees in engineering. Once attaining the
necessary credentials, he moved quickly through the ranks of the Khrunichev
hierarchy until in 1975, at the age of thirty-seven, he became the youngest
Director General in the history of Khrunichev. Kiselev's intimate knowledge
of the plant and its people, his personal experience in all levels of operations,
made him a formidable manager. His humble beginnings, hardscrabble life
story, and political acumen made him a fearsome and cunning competitor –
and a street-smart politician.

The opportunities of post-Soviet Russia were tailor-made for the skills,
experience, and initiative of Kiselev, and he eagerly took advantage. He was an
early Yeltsin supporter and confidant. Like Kiselev, Yeltsin had ascended to the
top ranks of Soviet elite from earthy, Russian peasant origins. While Yeltsin
and Kiselev understood the highly controlled Communist structure of party
and country, they shared the cultural characteristics of the average Russian man:
they ate and drank with gusto, loved to hunt and fish, and conducted themselves
as if life was short and should be lived to the fullest without regret. They eagerly
and unashamedly indulged all senses and appetites. There was more than one
instance when, in the midst of serious business meetings with Lockheed Martin
senior management, Anatoly would either miss a formal dinner or leave within
an hour to attend to "personal" business.

Kiselev had achieved a coup in 1993 when he outmaneuvered his aerospace
contemporaries in the privatization of Soviet industry by convincing the Yeltsin
administration to form Khrunichev Space and Research Center from the two
largest Soviet space enterprises, Khrunichev General Machine Building and KB
Salyut Design Bureau. His platform was an exclusive club called "The Presidential Club," a small group of people important to Yeltsin who had special
access to the President and his officials. Kiselev shared Yeltsin's suspicion of the
Ministry of General Machine Building, the elite Design Bureaus, and even the
Soviet Academy of Sciences – all of whom were implicated in the August 1991
coup against Mikhail Gorbachev and reformers like Yeltsin. Kiselev argued that,
with the end of the Cold War, Russia would neither require the extensive war
machine that had developed over decades nor could it afford the high technol-

ogy space enterprises it had used for propaganda purposes in the battle of ideology. Hence, rather than organizing the industry as it had in the past into Design Bureaus and General Machine Building Plants controlled by central planners, academicians, and party apparatchiks, it should be organized to best support the aerospace enterprise in the new realities of competition and free markets.

We never knew whether it was the force of Kiselev's arguments or the attractiveness of other considerations that persuaded Yeltsin and his team to give Kiselev so much authority and consolidated industrial capability.[39] By doing so, however, Yeltsin created a space behemoth and effectively vaulted Kiselev over his main competitor, Yuri Semenov of RSC Energia. That organization had been drastically downsized during the same period due to the spin-off of the rocket engine giant, Energomash, and its director Boris Katorgin, as well as the dispatch of the KB Saylut Design Bureau to Khrunichev, leaving Semenov and RSC Energia with the remnants of the Soviet manned space program, the Soyuz launch vehicle and manned capsule and the critical liquid fueled and final launch vehicle upper stage called the Block DM. The Block DM was the final or upper stage of the Proton vehicle; it autonomously maneuvered satellites to final destinations in orbit, softly releasing them in stable positions or trajectories. With the new Khrunichev established, Kiselev knew exactly what he wanted to do: enter the global commercial space marketplace with perhaps the Soviet Union's only value-added product that possessed real market potential – the massive and proven Proton launch vehicle with the Block DM upper-stage.[40]

IV

"MILK THE COW, BUT DO NOT PULL OFF THE UDDER."

Greek Proverb

As was customary, Anatoly began the meeting that day with a review of the Proton program. He enumerated the manifest for the next year, noting the new orders for commercial launch services garnered by ILS and the potential for additional missions should the market require them. He was very candid about the government manifest for Proton, which had dwindled since 1998 with the economic crash. He was always pressing for more orders, asking for funds to support expanding the production, processing, and launch capability of Proton.

But today, Anatoly focused on the new cryogenic upper stage, designed for the Proton by Khrunichev: the Brez M. This upper stage would give the Proton a new fourth and final stage launcher that could insert satellites into precise orbits at precise locations in space where they could operate for as many as fifteen years. Kiselev's plan was to substitute the Brez M for the RSC Energia Block DM currently in service. Kiselev lectured that the Brez M would be more reliable, flexible, and powerful than the Block DM, and with proper funding it would be ready for service within a year. Kiselev wanted Lockheed Martin to partially fund production of the Brez M and he wanted ILS to introduce the new upper stage to the marketplace, booking orders and collecting advances immediately. Both of these topics made for hard discussions. First, by statute, US investment in foreign ballistic missile technology development or "brokering such funding" for its investment is strictly prohibited and enforced with severe fines and criminal penalties.[41] We explained to Anatoly that there were no exceptions to this policy. In addition, the commercial telecommunications market – which, by 2000, like the tech bubble, was in sharp decline – had little capacity or appetite for new versions of launch vehicles. Kiselev had little tolerance for any of this line of argument, especially regarding US statutes, because regulations in Russia were flexible and subject to ad hoc waiver. I am convinced that Kiselev believed, like Khrunichev, Lockheed Martin could maneuver around regulations if it wanted to and was simply hiding behind the regulations to avoid investing in this new technology. We were adamant that these restrictions were firm and unmovable, were strictly enforced, and could put the entire corporation in jeopardy. However attractive the commercial launch business was to us at the time, it was trivial compared with the corporate and personal risks associated with violation of US law. As regards commercial markets, we constantly reminded Anatoly that the market is demand driven, not command driven, and that the current market conditions were such that rather than paying a *premium* for new (unproven) launch technology, commercial customers would expect large and persistent *discounts* for the additional risk they perceived they would be taking. As usual, the tenacity and emotion of Anatoly's line of argument reflected his conviction, but also other, unspoken considerations. In this case, we were to find that Anatoly had already made a Soviet-type commitment to the new Putin administration that Khrunichev would design, produce, and field a new upper stage for their national launch program at little or no cost to the government.   Kiselev was relishing the prospect of eliminating his competitor, Yuri Semenov and RSC Energia, from the commercial partnership. Anatoly was not subtle, nuanced, or particularly friendly in stating his case. It was jarring and somewhat unpleasant, especially for the most senior managers of Lockheed Martin, who were not used to this kind of badgering.

We were, however, getting a rare glimpse into the "strong man" management style of Soviet Communism. Over the next year, and at a discount, we were able to introduce the Brez M into the marketplace and eventually we were able to come to an accommodation with the US Congress and the State Department on compensation for the marketing rights to the Brez M. Lockheed Martin was allowed to amend its marketing agreement with Khrunichev to include the Brez M upper stage for additional and specifically enumerated consideration. We made it clear to Khrunichev that we were investing in neither the development nor the production of the Brez M, but, compensating Khrunichev for including the Brez M in our overall exclusive rights to the commercial Proton.[42]

The meeting that day concluded with a call from the office of Yuri Koptiev, head of the Russian Space Agency (RSA), confirming our meeting with Koptiev in an hour. We left Khrunichev and caravanned to RSA headquarters. Kiselev's chauffeured BMW led the entourage with a flashing blue police light perched on the roof. I asked one of his senior managers travelling with us how it was that Kiselev merited such an official apparatus. I was told that it was common in Moscow and, like so many other things, "available for a price". Apparently Anatoly was good friends with Moscow mayor Yuri Luzhkov and had made necessary arrangements to possess police equipment.

Arriving at the Russian Space Agency, we passed through large metal gates, where complete vehicle searches and credential checks are made just off the main street. Like the Khrunichev headquarters, the Russian Space Agency is housed in a large, multistory concrete building with little or no architectural charm or ornamentation. Concrete and steel were the construction materials of choice and large rectangles were the repetitive design elements of the anonymous utilitarian architecture of Soviet Communism. Once again, all manner of vehicles were in the parking area that adjoined the Space Agency building. Drivers leaned against their vehicles, smoked, and engaged one another in conversation; large men in dark coats loitered on the steps and in the doorway of the building, where uniform security guards reviewed us. The Russians seemed to have little patience for these necessary measures, though, and regarded each encounter with security personnel as a negotiation and an affront. We were whisked through the dark, cold, and largely empty lobby of the building to a small elevator that barely held five or six people, necessitating several trips to accommodate the top leadership of Khrunichev and Lockheed Martin.

We arrived on the fifth floor, which was somewhat brighter and warmer than the spare lobby below and which housed offices with wood paneled doorways and carpeting on the floor. It was not particularly busy that evening, but as it was almost 7:00pm we were impressed that so many personnel were still in their offices. Down the hall. after a sharp turn to the left, we entered the outer office of the Director General of Rosaviacosmos, Yuri Koptiev.

The offices of the Director General were grand. The ceiling must have been fifteen feet high and the room was large and well lit by an enormous crystal chandelier hanging at the center of the room. A large carved wood map of the world adorned one wall and thick wallpapering covered the rest. In the center of the room was a glass case containing large models of various launch vehicles and spacecraft, both in service and planned. Around the central model stand was a series of leather benches affording seating for twenty or thirty people. There was a large television in the corner of the room with CNN Headline News playing. When we entered the room we were somewhat surprised to see dozens of people loitering and smoking in the outer office.

As we shed the coats, hats, and gloves we had worn into the building, we noticed several individuals who had connections with our business. Our initial impression was that this was just a coincidence. Of course, it wasn't. We saw our old friend Alexy Krasnov, Deputy Chief of the International Division at Rosaviacosmos, formerly the science and technology attaché at the Soviet embassy in Washington. Also present was Mikail Tupolov, a Russian entrepreneur who had visited with ILS and Lockheed Martin managers on one or two occasions at conferences, offering his services as a consultant to represent us with Rosaviacosmos. Precisely what services he was offering was never quite clear, and consequently we never engaged him in any capacity. Anatoly appeared uncharacteristically stiff and a little nervous in this setting. He kept us together and aside, although Krasnov and Tupolov strolled by and offered greetings and took one or another of us aside to chat about our visit. Anatoly was tense during each encounter. Although Rosaviacosmos was nominally the government agency in charge of Russian aerospace industry and government space acquisition and operations, Khrunichev, through the maneuverings of

Kiselev, had a separate and unique charter issued by Presidential Decree making him accountable directly to the President, not to Koptiev. Koptiev and RSA acknowledged this arrangement, but clearly didn't like it. Tonight Anatoly, with his American "golden goose" on his arm, was attempting to enlist the aid of a senior government official (who viewed him with some skepticism) to urge Lockheed Martin to make an investment in new technology that would primarily benefit Khrunichev. Obviously there were many things going on behind the scenes about which we knew nothing – and perhaps that was best.

Two large double doors at the end of the room opened and a flurry of paper-clutching personnel in shirtsleeves emerged, talking quickly and loudly. They shot straight across the room to the exit and the Director General, Yuri Koptiev appeared. Koptiev is an enormous man, tall and broad and of generous proportions. He filled the doorway with his presence and Anatoly whisked us into his office.

Koptiev's office was as large as the waiting room. His walls were filled with photographs, commissions, decorations, and models. His desk was a hodgepodge of paperwork and old Cold War phones, a red one, a green one, and a black one. On one side of the room was an enormous ornate table that could easily seat twenty people and it was at this table that we each greeted Koptiev, whom we had met before on several occasions. He was friendly, but distinctly reserved, after all, we had no formal relationship with him or his office and yet were providing hundreds of millions of dollars a year to Khrunichev through our commercial launch business.

Kiselev began the proceedings by discussing the Brez M. Krunichev's new upper stage would be a vast improvement over the Block DM then in service. Unlike the DM, which could "burn" only twice when in orbit, the Brez M could fire as many as twenty times once in space. More importantly, unlike the Block DM, which initiated "burns" or firings as a result of command software loaded onto the vehicle, the Brez M included both onboard software and the capacity to be commanded directly from stations on the ground. Kiselev noted that several of the Proton failures over the previous ten years were a result of the Block DM not firing as planned for a second time in a satellite mission, leaving the payload in a useless orbit and resulting in a total business loss. Should such an event occur with the Brez M, Kiselev argued, ground controllers

could repeat the command for additional burns and recover from a failed ignition. Kiselev also made the case that the Brez M was a result of new, lighter,
and more advanced technology, and used propellants that were more environ-
mentally friendly and easier to store and handle. While the Brez M was still in
development, he felt we could have this capability within a year with additional
funding.

Yuri Koptiev began by talking about the state of the Russian space program. He said there was no denying that efforts had slowed as a consequence
of the economic crisis in the past year. He added, however, that the space program remained an important priority for the new Putin presidency and that
resources, however constrained, would continue to flow to critical projects. He
discussed the importance of the partnerships formed with American aerospace
companies, like Lockheed Martin and International Launch Services, in providing commercial work for Russian industry and the efficient utilization of
Russian assets for US initiatives, like the Space Station. He said cooperation
such as in the commercial launch business and development of the International Space Station were positive and prudent for all concerned.

We asked specifically about the ability to make payrolls in several space
industries, as we had heard rumors that companies were not making subcontract payments to suppliers. We worried this could cause supply disruptions,
schedule delays, and contract defaults that would ultimately undermine the
business and our relationships. Koptiev said he had heard the same things, but
felt confident that Russian companies would honor their commitments and
that we would experience no disruptions, delays, or defaults. His words were
reassuring, but his lack of detail in explaining precisely how this was to be
avoided left us uneasy.

Koptiev then addressed the Brez M specifically. He said it was initiated as a
government program, originally designed during the Cold War as part of their
planetary exploration program, but that it would be a useful and improved
upper stage for the launch of telecommunications satellites into geosynchro-
nous orbits. We had speculated internally that the Brez M, with its enhanced
maneuverability, multi-start engine, and both autonomous and commanded
operations was more likely an advanced anti-satellite weapon than a planetary
probe. Nevertheless, it *was* an improvement over the Block DM in terms of

cost and performance on nominal commercial telecommunications missions. Koptiev said that the Russian government had funded the Brez M and that it would eventually be completed for service in the Russian space program. However, it could be brought into service much more rapidly and beneficially to all if it were to receive an additional investment of funds from Lockheed Martin.

As we had at Khrunichev, we informed Koptiev of the US laws that imposed strict prohibitions against investing in the development of ballistic missile technologies in foreign countries and why that meant that we could not invest in the development of the Brez M. We inquired as to why Khrunichev itself might not invest its returns from the ILS business into this project, as the general economic model would indicate. Of course we had no insight into how funds were distributed within Khrunichev, its suppliers, or the Russian government, although it was patently clear to us that the name of the game was to extract as much capital as possible from western partners, regardless of the details of how the funds were used or invested.

We were engaging in a kabuki dance that, over the years, was ritualistically observed in this relationship. The Russians couched requests for additional funds in terms that included the elements of standard business propositions (marketing plans, demand forecasts, competitor assessments) but resisted attempts to explore alternative business possibilities with detailed resource allocation models aimed at maximizing returns. In short, we had no idea how Khrunichev actually used the resources they received from the partnership and, therefore, we had no basis for assessing investment efficiency or quality. For this reason, our business arrangements were always simple and straightforward. This was an irritant to Kiselev and his compatriots as it seemed as if there was some cipher for the unlocking of our wallets that had only to be found and employed, to be rewarded with indiscriminate largesse. Kiselev was not without justification in clinging to this idea as the history of the relationship between Lockheed Martin and Khrunichev provided ample evidence that such behavior was indeed possible. Whether by cultural misunderstanding, lack of a common language of commerce, superior negotiating strategy, overly optimistic market forecasts, or simple management incompetence, Lockheed Martin had showered Khrunichev with hundreds of millions of dollars in cash and advance payments in the early days of the relationship, with little or no formal accounting.

As our experience grew and as the telecommunications bubble of the late '90s deflated, we pulled back on cash transfers to Khrunichev, explaining that prior advances had to cover current costs. Kiselev and his team consistently looked for the keys to the past and a return to the "open wallet" policies of the '90s.

Koptiev listened carefully, but implacably. He slowly smoked a cigarette, looking a bit like Sydney Greenstreet in an old Humphrey Bogart film. He turned to the Proton manifest for 2001 and the challenging spring before us: six launches scheduled in nine weeks, culminating with the launch of the first element of the International Space Station in July. We all agreed that it was an enormous challenge ahead and pledged to work hard and together to make it a success. Kiselev seemed relieved to conclude the meeting.

Leaving the Russian space agency in a light snow and with traffic beginning to thin, we sped our way to the outskirts of the city to a restaurant that had become the traditional ILS partners' dining locale: The Tsar's Hunt.

As our caravan pulled off the highway onto a frontage road, we could see through the snow a familiar two-story log structure, like an alpine ski chalet, in the middle of what looked like a somewhat run-down suburban US strip mall. It had a long awning leading from the parking area that was littered with the usual dark BMW and Mercedes sedans, with drivers leaning on the cars or sitting inside them smoking. We shuttled into the lodge and were greeted by young men and women dressed in "Cossack" garb, complete with high-buttoned, muslin peasant shirts, large belts, and high leather boots. The "Hunt" was decorated with hunting trophies on the walls, animal skin rugs on the floors, and rustic finished wood stairs, walls, and railings. There was a din of high energy, traditional music played by a small string and balalaika ensemble near the large, roaring stone fireplace. Everyone loosened their ties and shed their jackets as we made our way up the open stairwell to the large table in the center of the perch upstairs, overlooking the main floor.

Servers were already at the table, armed with cups of the traditional sweet Russian wheat beverage Kvass – like iced tea, only more viscous – and, of course, the omnipresent bottles of chilled vodka were placed at strategic stations along the table. No sooner had we taken our seats than the toasting began. Anatoly, as the dean of the delegation, began with an earnest toast to our historic partnership, our friendship, and to the future of our enterprise. His manner was serious and formal, and he paused for effect between each injunction. He spoke of the future and the need for trust between us. Then pulling up his shoulders, he contorted his face into a gnomish smile, and raised his right hand, placing his index finger and thumb less than an inch apart from one another. "With just a little help from our friends at Lockheed Martin," he said, "we will dominate the world market with the Proton and the Brez M!"

As was customary, the evening included many more toasts and many jokes. The Russians are especially fond of animal parables told time and again to the uproarious laughter of all. We frequently traded Cold War stories and gently debated old contentions, like ballistic missile defense. On this point it is interesting to note that the Russians freely admitted the US pursuit of the strategic defense imitative was "the last straw" in breaking the back of the Soviet regime – a back that had already been deeply weakened by the war with Afghanistan and further undermined by the restiveness in the Eastern European republics. They experienced that weakness firsthand in the decline in the level of spending on advanced aerospace activities over the decade before the fall of the Berlin Wall. The Buran space shuttle program was cancelled, programs like the Brez M were stretched out indefinitely, plans to build additional launch infrastructure in the northern complex at Plesestk were delayed, and even necessary maintenance at the primary launch complex at Baikenour was curtailed. They consistently were asked to do more with less and they cut corners where they could to make ends meet. They could see the decline of the Soviet state and they recalled their discussions of how they would survive in a post-Soviet Russia. They had watched and encouraged plans for cooperation in space between the United States and the Soviet Union as a potential bridge into an uncertain future. They described how the "serial" plants of the general machine building enterprises functioned as mini-civic entities that provided not only jobs for thousands of employees, but also housing, education, recreational activities, and pensions. A Director General like Anatoly Kiselev was much more than a plant manager; he was the mayor, the leader, the breadwinner for an enterprise of 30,000 people, all of whom looked to him and his management team for everything in their lives. We were absolutely mesmerized by this intimate look into Communist feudalism and the isolation and utter dependence under which the average

Soviet citizen lived, even those with advanced educations and highly technical skills.

The relevance of all this to our enterprise was crystal clear. The cash from commercial launch services, the advance payments and reservations for future launch services that we funneled into Khrunichev, was now funding this enormous enterprise. We were not only fueling investments in long delayed modernized technology developments, we were supporting thousands of technicians and engineers and their families, *and* we were probably funding indirectly a significant portion of the sustained activities of the entire Russian space agency.

These evenings were always enjoyable and relaxed. We were good friends as well as good partners. And yet, despite this the Russians remained mysterious — a complex amalgam of happiness and darkness, joyously living for today while harboring deep skepticism and suspicion about the future. They were light hearted, but heavy handed, trusting, but endlessly scheming. They could be sentimental, yet capable of brutal behavior. I'm not sure we ever *really* knew them.

———

Early the next morning we met Anatoly at the office of the Deputy Prime Minister for Defense Industry, Iilya Klebanov. We had specifically asked for a meeting to discuss concerns about the stability of the Russian aerospace subcontract community and rumors we consistently heard that payrolls were not being met and that deliveries of critical components might be in jeopardy. Uncharacteristically, the meeting was arranged for us by the US embassy. Normally our meetings in Moscow were arranged by our partners at Khrunichev, but because of the seniority of Minister Klebanov and the nature of our interest, we thought it better to have Ambassador Jim Collins make the arrangements himself. As we were to later find, there also was tension between Klebanov and Kiselev since Klebanov was specifically given a charge by the new President Putin to consolidate the more than 100 separate entities that comprised the Russian defense industry—which meant that Anatoly's empire at Khrunichev was potentially at risk. Throughout the time of our partnership, we consistently heard rumors of consolidation, first within Russia alone and then later with elements of aerospace in Ukraine.

The Prime Minister's offices are located in the Russian White House, a large, looming structure that stands out against both the ornate Stalinist "wedding cakes" of the mid-twentieth century and the sterile concrete bunkers of the '60s and '70s. It is an imposing white complex that looks, from a distance, like a vast hospital. Inside, the facilities were more modern and well appointed than the other governmental offices to which we were accustomed. The hallways were large, with art on the walls; the offices were paneled in wood and decorated with fine furniture.

Along with the US Ambassador, we waited for Anatoly in the hallway outside Klebanov's office. Soon Anatoly's hulking figure and booming voice appeared down the hallway as he walked toward us, talking with members of his staff. We greeted one another and waited for the Deputy Prime Minister's assistant to show us into his office. While we waited, another figure appeared in the hallway, walking fast and loudly talking on a cell phone. He was a stocky man with a large black leather overcoat and matching cap that looked straight off an old Bolshevik poster. He spied Anatoly Kiselev and marched straight to his side, grabbing him by both arms and kissing him on either cheek. An animated conversation took place between the two and Kiselev, looking a bit sheepish and put out, pulled the man to the side, where a short and intense conversation transpired. I asked our interpreter what that was all about and he explained that the man was Yury Luzhkov, Mayor of Moscow, and he was buttonholing Kiselev to attend a fundraiser for him the following week. He was badgering Kiselev to "buy" a table, or perhaps two. We kidded Anatoly that this scene was very familiar to us from our time in Washington: politicians around the world seemed to share a common need and apparent relish in shaking money from associates.

Soon we were escorted in to Klebanov's office. He was polite and proper and well prepared, expressing good knowledge of our partnership and business activities. At Anatoly's specific request, and not without a lack of conviction, we told Klebanov about our satisfaction with the partnership both financially and professionally. We discussed the market and how the two vehicles we offered, the Atlas and the Proton, worked together to capture a greater share of the commercial space launch market than either could independently. We expressed great confidence and trust in Khrunichev, but said we were concerned about the financial health of subcontract elements of the Russian aerospace industry and the impact that delays or cancellations could have on our business.

Klebanov began with a lengthy discussion of the current limitations on government expenditures due to the economic circumstances in Russia. He said that President Putin was working hard to establish economic order, enforce tax collections, and stem the outflow of capital from the country. He said these measures would take time, but would correct the situation. The defense and aerospace industry was important to Russia and he was looking hard at problems and opportunities. Klebanov said that he understood our concerns and confirmed that, in isolated instances and for short durations, some industries experienced stress and that some short-term gaps were possible. On the other hand, he said he and his office would make sure that these temporary and isolated instances would not result in critical delays or cancellations. He asked Anatoly to personally advise him of any potential difficulties in supply and promised that he would address them in a timely fashion.

Klebanov remarked that cooperation between the US and Russia in both commercial and governmental space activities was a positive development and helpful to maintaining stability in their industry. We agreed that dangerous proliferation of missile technology was in neither country's interest and that these partnerships added confidence that there would be no escapements even during this economic crisis.

As with all of the senior Russian officials with whom we met, there was a complex mixture of necessity, genuine partnership, and endurance of circumstance that was in Klebanov's tone, words, and posture. After the Cold War, Russians had been lectured, cajoled, and to some extent condescended to by American politicians, academicians, and now business partners. The weight of that, in addition to dire financial circumstances that necessitated a patient acceptance of the situation, was wearing many Russian officials thin. There were never any overt signals of a chaffing in these meetings, but I couldn't help but sense a strained endurance of this intrusion into what were clearly perceived as private Russian matters. In hindsight, it should have been clear to us that over time the Russians would gravitate towards a rise of nationalistic independence that was so central to the Putin presidency.

V

THE LAUNCH

"There shall be wings! If the accomplishment be not for me, 'tis for some other. The spirit cannot die; and man, who shall know all and shall have wings. . ."
Leonardo da Vinci

The next morning we left at dawn for the flight to Baikenour in Kazakhstan. Lockheed Martin Air Operations had long since prohibited the corporate Gulfstream V from landing at the Baikenour airfield after an earlier experience revealed inadequate support and maintenance facilities at the field. We therefore made the journey to the launch site on a chartered Tupolev-134A, a Russian long-range passenger aircraft that had, since 1967, served as the backbone of the Russian civil airline fleet. The airplane was made by the legendary Tupolev OKB organization, which had also developed and constructed the Cold War stalwart TU-16, the strategic bomber we called "the Badger."

The plane was comfortably updated with new interior furnishings and piloted by western crews. As we boarded the aircraft, the traditional Tupolev glass nose reflected the glare of the morning sun and reminded us that we were boarding Russian hardware. We lifted off from the runway and the plane eased south-eastward, towards the sunlight and central Asia.

It was nearly afternoon when we descended into the high desert of Kazakhstan. My first impression of this vista was how strikingly similar it is to the high desert geography of Edwards Air Force Base in California. Test pilots with "the right stuff" loved these dry, barren expanses, calling them "heaven's gates." That day in Baikenour, snow was on the ground, sparse and scattered in patches across the brown, brush-strewn landscape. There were no trees and only small hills. It was desolate, dry, and vast, the same landscape extended endlessly in all directions. In the distance we saw the familiar cosmodrome facilities of weathered and worn steel and concrete, with gantry towers like oil derricks dotting the complex. At the time, the Baikenour cosmodrome was technically owned by the Kazakhstan government, but it was controlled by the Russian Federation. For decades it had been the secret Soviet space complex Turytam. I was reminded of a quip by John McMahon, a Lockheed Martin executive and former Deputy Director of the Central Intelligence Agency, when he was asked on his first tour of the Kremlin whether he had ever seen the Kremlin before – he paused and said, "Well, not from this angle." We had seen Turytam many times before.

The approach to the enormous airstrip at Baikenour is fascinating. As the TU-134A gently banked around to the airstrip itself, I could see the runway – one enormous concrete pad three or four times the width of a normal runway and at least three times the length. We learned on earlier visits that this facility was constructed for the landing of the Soviet space shuttle, the Buran or "Snowstorm", which flew only once, in 1988. In 2000, in a large "mothball" facility at the cosmodrome, we were given a tour of the Buran's flight hardware and a mock-up of its enormous Energia launch system. Although it was largely abandoned and clearly in ill repair, we had little indication that inattention to the facility itself would cause the building to collapse two years later, in 2002, killing eight people and destroying the shuttle and the mock-up of the Energia rocket. Such was the state of dilapidation of much of the cosmodrome. As we touched down on the runway, we could easily see the disrepair in the concrete slabs. Large cracks buckled the runway, with grasses pushing up between the openings. As we bumped and bounced down the runway we were reminded of why Lockheed Martin Air Operations refused to take the corporate Gulfstream to this facility. We taxied past a small hut the only visible structure on the enormous concrete island, and spotted the buses parked and ready to take us to the hotel to which we would retire before the launch of the Proton vehicle later that night. The temperature was -10 degrees Centigrade (14 degrees Fahrenheit) and the wind chill made it feel like -20 Centigrade. We were informed that at the time of launch, just before 1:00am, it would be -20 Centigrade and the wind chill would make it feel like -30 Centigrade (almost 10 below in Fahrenheit). We traveled light since we would be in Baikenour for less than twenty-four hours, but our supplies included arctic gear especially provided for launch observation. Even momentary exposure to such cold and wind literally took your breath away.

We disembarked and walked directly to the open-air hut, where Kazakh officials sat in large green coats and fur lined hats festooned with Soviet-style medals that seemed to be made of tin. They had a table that looked like it was out of an old western telegraph office, with scraps of paper strewn about. Our passports were examined, as were our visas for entry and exit from Kazakhstan. Removing the small slips of visa paper from our passports to present to the officials could not be accomplished with bulky gloves and so our bare hands quickly froze. It was lost on no one that, should this little scrap of paper be mislaid in the ensuing eighteen hours, no departure from Baikenour would be possible. No one mislaid the papers. The papers were ceremoniously stamped with authority, and with a slight grunt we were ushered onto the busses that would take us to the Polyot Hotel where we would rest, have dinner, and wait for the launch that night.

The ride to the Polyot was as bumpy and hazardous as the landing at the airfield. Buildings, abandoned and deteriorating, littered the sides of the roads, with rail lines leading nowhere running alongside. Power and telephone poles stripped of wire looked like crucifixes lining the empty streets. Just as at the airport in Moscow, little care or attention seemed to be paid to outmoded, obsolete, unused facilities and equipment. They were simply abandoned – unused, unattended, disintegrating. The little mortar and cinderblock ghost towns were punctuated by long stretches of high desert emptiness. Incredibly, large yaks and camels, with their distinctive long wooly coats, grazed in the distance, completely unconcerned as we drove by.

We soon arrived at the Polyot Hotel, a small two-story lodge structure within a compound of buildings that housed engineers and technicians who worked at the cosmodrome. It was a modest facility, home not only for launch visitors, like us, but to the crews who had been there for the past thirty days of the launch campaign. We made our way to our rooms, where we took off our many external layers and rested from the day's journey. I was almost immediately interrupted by our chief engineer announcing that we were to have a final launch readiness review with the customer, Sirius Satellite Radio, the satellite manufacturer, Space Systems Loral, and Khrunichev at T-6 hours — which was in thirty minutes.

We convened in the hotel conference room and mission managers from each of the organizations that had been in Baikenour for the entire launch campaign briefed us on the status of the launch vehicle, the spacecraft, and the ground support systems. Each team carefully reviewed the status of its component and, at the end, our program director reported that all systems were nominal for a launch at 1:59am, December 1, local Baikenour time.

Weeks earlier, the 12,000-pound Sirius 3 spacecraft was flown by Russia's behemoth Antinov aircraft, the largest aircraft in the world, from Palo Alto, California to Baikenour, where waiting launch crews from ILS and Space Systems Loral carefully unloaded the delicate instrument from the yawning open mouth of the giant airplane. Once fully checked out and readied, the spacecraft had been mated to the Block DM upper stage of the Proton. The pair was then stacked on the horizontally-stored Proton vehicle that had been shipped by railcar to Baikenour months earlier. Then, just days before, the Proton, with its payload onboard, was rolled to the launch pad and slowly erected into vertical launch position. Now the launch vehicle was being fueled with liquid oxygen and liquid kerosene (the hydrogen propellant) and the resultant 500,000 pounds of controlled explosive was gradually and carefully readied for launch. The massive vehicle stood on the pad, with almost $300 million of total value onboard and we were less than five hours to launch. Just two hours after launch we would either unlock all of this value for a decade or more of operations or lose it forever. They say space is not for the faint of heart.

As the technical teams returned to their command positions at the launch site, we retired to the Polyot for a dinner consisting of traditional Russian and Kazakhstan cuisine, heavy on oily cold fish, very marbled sausages, and, of course, vodka. A few hours of rest and we were awakened for the short journey to the launch viewing site.

The night was eerily cold and silent, with not a cloud in the sky. The stars glistened and twinkled through the sub-zero temperatures. There is almost no ground clutter of light in Baikenour and the sky was completely full of stars, layer after layer. I recalled being at the Hughes Space and Communications plant in Los Angeles years earlier, being briefed by a young engineer who described the capability of a proposed space-based infrared sensor. He said that the instrument they were designing could track thousands of ballistic missile reentry vehicles simultaneously and update their trajectories in milliseconds. As I pondered this seemingly impossible task, he said, "Think about looking up at the stars with the naked eye on a cloudless night with little or no ground clutter to interfere. There will be about three thousands stars visible as you look skyward...now imagine each star moving towards you at hundreds of miles an hour...finding, tracking, and targeting these objects is our challenge." As I gazed skyward that night I thought about "three thousand stars" as the clouds of my frozen breath, looking like little galaxies, slowly rose into the sky. Our ride to the viewing site was silent. It was near midnight and the crunching of the tires on the frozen road was the only sound that was heard.

The Proton viewing complex at Baikenour – located in the middle of nowhere – is a cozy log structure with a broad and open porch. Heaters were blowing inside and a table of snacks was laid before us, with the obligatory bottles of vodka placed about. We had an open telephone line to the launch command center and could follow the progress of the launch process as translated by our team. First we heard the short Russian commands followed by English translation. As we had learned years earlier, the American custom of a launch count down was not universally adopted. Russian protocol, for example, is to determine a launch time and then simply to proceede to launch at the mark. Our Russian partners considered the bother with "T-minus X," "hold for this and that," and resetting the launch clock for a new T-0 a curious and somewhat melodramatic concoction. Nevertheless, our commercial enterprise and the expectations of our western customers required a customary count down and so the Russians obliged, although somewhat haphazardly and rarely with a good match between count down and actual launch. Part of this is cultural and part is a result of the kinds of engineering inherent in Russian and American space launch systems. Americans have, by and large, developed relatively fragile launch vehicles, launched from benign and highly controlled environments in Florida and California, where performance margins right at the edge are tolerated. Russians vehicles, on the other hand, operate from the remote and harsh environments of Baikenour and Plesetsk, where temperatures could vary from tens of degrees below zero in the winter to over 110 degrees in the summer. Russian computer capabilities consistently lagged with respect to the US and thus heavy internal automation was always onboard, necessitating much more powerful propulsion systems. At the Cape, winds over 20 knots are a constant launch constraint, whereas in Baikenour, vehicles are routinely launched in gales exceeding 40 knots. As a consequence, Russian launch vehicles are heartier and more resistant to small variances. This is not to suggest that Russian vehicles are superior to American vehicles simply that they were designed to different tolerances and thus required different technologies. To be sure, we experienced launch scrubs in Baikenour and had had our share of failures, but we rarely had the customary "on again, off again" delays common to the American way to space.

In this case the launch operations went especially smoothly: tanks were filled and topped off, batteries were charged, power was smoothly transferred from the ground to the spacecraft itself, communication links were confirmed, and in what seemed like no time at all we left the warm confines of the lodge and stepped onto the porch, into the wind and the cold that felt like walking into a glass wall. I find it interesting that when you step into heat from a cool room you warm up slowly and the heat is embracing. Only moments later does it becomes close and then stultifying. Whereas stepping into truly frigid air, regardless of how warm you are, hits you like a club and chills to the bone within seconds.

We stood looking out onto the vast, dark emptiness of the Kazakhstan high desert, punctuated only by the klieg light on the distant launch vehicle and gantry. The scene was vaguely reminiscent of *2001: A Space Odyssey*. The Proton stood fuming, as if breathing, straining at its bonds; ready to leap into the sky. The speakers attached to the lodge blared alternating loud monotone Russian commands followed by English translations.

"All power has been switched to internal."

And then the count down, first in Russian, then English: "Three, two, one... ignition, lift off!"

There is something profound, even primal, about the launch of a large space vehicle, especially at night. The billowing smoke and faint light that starts upon ignition, the almost blinding light as the first stage hammers away at the launch pad like an avenging angel. Slowly at first and then faster and faster it rises up, carving a bright twinkling arc in the sky as the Earth rotates beneath its flight.... And then the *basso profundo* sound that crawls along the ground like a snarling beast, moving at a fraction of the speed of the light, until finally the concussive force of the air pressure from the enormous explosion imprints on your body the events of just moments ago.

As the vehicle rises into the black sky and the light of the engines narrows to the tiniest pin prick of shimmering brightness, the trajectory seems to flatten out — a trick of perspective, almost as if the vehicle were going parallel to the Earth rather than straight up. All eyes strain to see the last flickers of the engines as the vehicle slips into the firmament, already nearly five hundred miles down range and over one hundred miles in altitude speeding ahead at almost 13,000 miles per hour. It has escaped Earth orbit and is streaking towards a position nearly one-tenth the distance to the Moon.

The jubilant launch party burst through the doors of the lodge to the awaiting heaters, snacks, and, of course, vodka. I lingered on the porch, braced against the frigid air, and looked out upon the cosmodrome's launch complex. I thought about the incredible history of this vast desert that stood before me. This is where Sputnik, Ladka, Yuri Gagarin, the Mir space station, and the cosmonauts bravely tested the limits of endurance and courage — and some of them had paid the ultimate price. I thought about the Cold War ICBMs tested there and the hundreds of secret reconnaissance and test vehicles launched from these very pads. I thought how curious it was that the two great gateways from Earth to the stars should be almost exactly half-way around the world from one another — one in the middle of the central plains of Eurasia and the other in the warm, flat marshes of northern Florida. Two celestial bus stations, separated by space, and ideology, now joined in common purpose.

VI

A New Reality, and
New Possibilities

No sooner had we arrived back at the Polyot with a scant four hours to rest before we were scheduled to depart for the Baikenour airstrip, than one of our Russian partners informed me that I had been summoned to the Khrunichev dacha, only a few hundred yards from the Polyot.

The Khrunichev dacha at Baikenour was a heavily guarded building that served as the accommodations, dining hall, and recreational facility for Khrunichev and Strategic Rocket Forces leadership. It was a modern, Nordic-looking wood and steel structure with the appearance of an embassy residence. I was greeted at the door by General Ivanov, former head of the Soviet Strategic Rocket forces and now Deputy Director General of Khrunichev. General Ivanov was straight out of central casting, tall and weathered, with square Slavic features and short gray hair. He invited me upstairs to the formal dining room. The room was tastefully decorated with fine wood paneling, oriental rugs, and long drapes over the floor-to-ceiling windows at the far end. The carved wooden table was very large, capable of seating as many as twenty, and was laid with full stemware, silver, and fine china. The residence staff and passed glasses of beer and wine and, of course, vodka. As I entered the room I was introduced to special guests from Moscow – General Perminov of the Ministry of Defense, Chief of the Main Staff, and Deputy Commander in Chief of the Strategic Rocket Forces, and Colonel Nesterov, Chief of the Division on Launch and Ground Infrastructure from Rosaviacosmos, the Russian Space Agency.

Almost immediately the Khrunichev management team entered the room in high spirits. They were led by First Deputy Director Alexander Medvedev and included Igor Dodin, the cosmosdrome Chief of Operations for Khrunichev. There were enthusiastic warm greetings for all, although they carefully observed the ritualistic and superstitious avoidance of any congratulatory comments, as the final completion of the launch mission – spacecraft separation – was still an hour away. Unlike Anatoly Kiselev, First Deputy Medvedev was trained at the best Russian technical university and went directly from his PhD in aeronautical engineering to Khrunichev. He is the face of the "new Russia," and a protégé of the new President, Vladimir Putin. Medvedev is an earnest technician and sincere man, and in many ways unlike his Director, Anatoly Kiselev. Unbeknownst to us at the time, Kiselev was already in the process of retiring from Khrunichev and Alexander Medvedev would soon become the new Director General. Medvedev's moderation, steadiness, and modern interests were welcome departures from the unpredictable and mercurial behavior of Kiselev. Unfortunately, Medvedev's lack of Kiselev's political skills, his instinct for maneuvering and his ruthlessness, would prove to be shortcomings that left him unprepared for the rough and tumble of the new Russian economy, and eventually led to *his* ouster three years later.

I joined the dinner party for what I learned was a traditional, post-launch meal of many courses and varieties of food, with large quantities of wine, beer, and vodka dispensed and consumed. The conversation was genial and celebratory, but somewhat subdued. Obviously, the mission at hand was distracting all of us, as was the fact that so many in our party had not met before and as a consequence, we were initially reserved in one another's presence. All this changed, however, when an aide came into the room and whispered into Medvedev's ear. Alexander smiled broadly and leapt to his feet, offering a toast to the successful completion of the launch of the Sirius 3 satellite! At this point things became relaxed and informal, with many toasts and warm exchanges. War stories rolled out, including the story of the Soviet Army General who, having served in the artillery, was assigned to lead the relatively new Strategic Rocket Forces in the early 1970's. He had claimed that artillerymen "do not hide in bunkers" and so, despite clear warnings to the contrary, he had insisted on watching his first launch from field seats only a few dozen meters from the launch pad. When the rocket ignited, the shock, flames, and debris of the launch killed the entire viewing party.

"We in the Army have evolved," General Perminov deadpanned to the laughter of the entire party. "We now sit facing away from the blast!"

As the evening wore on, the topic of discussion, as usually happened in these circumstances, slowly turned to the Cold War and the history of space-based cooperation between the United States and Russia. All agreed that cooperation between the US and Russia was a good thing and that over the years it had served many useful purposes for both sides. Yet, despite this consensus, there was a sense conveyed that they were disappointed with the cooperative projects. I asked why?

The Russians at first demurred and waved off the implication that cooperation was not a pure good, but I pressed them and soon they opened up. They expressed disappointment with the scope and nature of space cooperation between Russia and the US. They said that government bureaucrats ran the projects on both sides and that those projects therefore lacked imagination, depth, and sustainability. One went so far as to call them "geopolitical stunts" aimed primarily at propping up the manned space programs in both countries and achieving very little that could not have been accomplished independently. They said that industry and the military had little influence over these projects and that, when they *did* participate, they were closely watched by government officials so that technology secrets, the true state of capabilities, and the health of industries could be protected or concealed.

I told them about my time in the White House during the Bush administration and how many Russian diplomats and academicians, all looking for cooperative space projects and encouraging space collaboration, had visited me. I had assumed that these "openings" were carefully staffed and coordinated, and that they reflected the thinking of the entire government. I explained that the space exploration initiative outlined by President Bush had as a specific goal the cooperation of US and Russian space experts aimed at offering important new focus to both aerospace communities. I had even participated in the meeting with General Secretary Gorbachev and Vice President Quayle when the General Secretary had specifically suggested that we start joint projects in space exploration. I asked why no industry leaders came and discussed projects. They told me that the academicians had been essentially "freelancing," hoping to enhance their personal prestige and clout in the teetering Soviet regime by attracting interest in show-piece projects and high level contacts in the US government. They complained that academicians had a long history of participation in global conferences during the Cold War, ostensibly to share scientific insights and advanced technologies, but primarily to learn and bring back new results to be exploited in the institutes and design bureaus. Only these academicians and professional diplomats with close ties to the old Soviet politburo had the freedom to travel to the US and elsewhere, and so only they could arrange appointments with senior officials in the White House, even in the final stages of the Soviet Union. Such contacts for members of the aerospace industry were, at the time, impossible.

They said that only after the Soviet Union had ceased to exist and American delegations came to Russia to establish direct and more open contacts did they have the opportunity to make contacts themselves. These initiatives, they noted, resulted in new ways of thinking and operating, creating enterprises that generated substantial resources for independent research and development projects. The Brez M is a good example, explained Medvedev. For a decade, this vehicle had been proposed to the Russian government for a variety of missions, including planetary exploration and other national security applications, but no resources to develop and deploy the vehicle ever materialized. Now, with the partnership between Lockheed Martin and the commercial launch vehicle business, the Brez M would be a reality, offering substantial and new capabilities not only for the market, but for future government projects as well. He said the new thinking in Russia and the United States resulted in innovative applications of Russian technology to American space design efforts. He observed that NASA administrator Dan Goldin's direct engagement with Boeing and Khrunichev for the modification and launch of the Zarya FGB control module as the first element of the International Space Station was done on a strictly engineer-to-engineer basis, with the governments bureaucrats by and large staying out of the way.

I said that the US aerospace industry was also benefitting substantially from industry-to-industry cooperation. For example, Lockheed Martin was developing a new launch vehicle for the government and commercial marketplace using Russian made RD-180 engines. These engines had better performance than any made in the United States, and the resulting vehicle, the Atlas V, a combination and integration of US and Russian space technology, was the most advanced, capable, and efficient in the world. It was an exciting time.

Both the American and Russian aerospace communities had been shaped by the Cold War and its end. Each had confronted a crisis, facing the potential end to the industry as they had known it for almost half a century. Circumstances had forced each to make adaptations and modifications, as well as painful reductions and consolidations. And yet, with the encouragement, but little interference, of the two governments, we had found some common ground in technology, in enterprise, and in a vision for the future that was a singular moment of progress. As I wearily made my way through the ice and snow back to the Polyot for a departure from Baikenour, now less than an hour away, I couldn't help but consider that someday the United States and Russia may again face each other as adversaries. My hope was that if that day came, deep inside new armories of Armageddon, a cadre of individuals who had known each other, had worked together, and had achieved mutual success with those of the other side just might make a difference.

VII

A WORLD TRANSFORMED

It was a long but relaxing flight from Moscow to Washington DC the day after the launch. As we retraced our path from Europe back to North America, following the great circle route first contemplated by astronomer Ptolemy almost two thousand years earlier, I thought about the fact that it had been almost twelve years since the Cold War ended. The United States still had forces in Europe and Asia, and now on the ground in Kosovo, Kuwait, and Saudi Arabia, and controlled a "no fly" zone over Iraq, which had invaded Kuwait in the summer of 1990. Iraq's invading forces were defeated and repelled by a large coalition of countries and forces acting in concert to contain and roll back that illegal invasion. General Chuck Hoerner, commander of the allied air forces, called operation Desert Storm the first "space war." Precision guided weapons, precision location, navigation and timing signals from GPS satellites allowing soldiers in the dust, sand, and dark to know their position and the position of other "blue forces" with pinpoint accuracy, real-time communications from satellites hovering thousands of miles above allowing instant and continuous mobile communications – with all of these, the hostile and unforgiving terrain of the desert became a transparent ocean to the allied forces who quickly outmatched and outgunned even the elite Iraqi Republican Guard. Several NSC meetings in late 1990, before the President's decision to form and lead the coalition to free Kuwait addressed potential causalities. At those meetings, General Colin Powell and the Joint Chiefs team soberly warned of at least 5,000 US causalities in the 500,000 troops combined arms operation. But owing to the incredible discipline, overwhelming force and, yes, application of space technology, there were less than 200.

In November 1992, President Bush was defeated for re-election by Governor Bill Clinton of Arkansas. Space exploration initiatives that started under the Bush administration in 1990 would eventually falter when incoming the Clinton administration replaced them with new objectives and new initiatives. The Departments of Defense and Energy would cement stronger ties and programmatic relationships with NASA, but they would not take a new and significant role in space exploration. The American aerospace industry would rapidly consolidate in the early '90s, at the specific request of the Department of Defense, which actually paid for their mergers and acquisition costs. The resulting integrated aerospace giants would flounder in the 1990s, trying their own form of "diversification" by entering into the adjacent and booming market of global telecommunications, resulting in another round of aerospace commercialization that Norm Augustine has repeatedly referred to as a record unblemished by success.

NASA would see plans for space exploration put on indefinite hold. The Space Station, that had consumed so much of the Agency's attention, energy, and political muscle, even at the expense of President Bush's more comprehensive vision for a long-term manned space effort, would be radically restructured, reduced, and reoriented, relying heavily, if not primarily, on outsourcing launch, power, core modules, and crew transfer and rescue capabilities to Russia. It is on orbit today, manned continuously since 2000 and still adding elements—nearly $100 billion in total cost and over twenty-five years in design and construction. The original 1983 cost estimate of $8B and anticipated completion date of 1998 have passed memory and relevance. It is what it is.

Funds for new, cutting edge technologies, like the National Aerospace Plane, dried up as real defense dollars continued to contract, despite the infusion from Desert Storm. NASA and DoD would return to old patterns of insolated infrastructure capitalization, and important initiatives, such as integrated national launch, and the benefits and efficiencies they offered would once again elude our grasp. Desert Storm would prove that the American way of war had changed forever. DoD space initiatives – from position, navigation, and timing, to weather, communications, and reconnaissance – would be rapidly accelerated in order to accommodate the force multiplication and discrimination opportunities of which Operation Desert Storm had only offered a glimpse. Getting more from less was an unexpected spin off of enhanced space capabilities and the necessities of modern warfare.

The National Space Council itself was disbanded by the Clinton administration, within a week of his inauguration, as part of a "streamlining" of White House operations. I noted with interest that the published "staff savings" associated with the elimination of the Space Council was eighty-four positions although we never had more than twelve people assigned directly to our activity. However, the Clinton administration did – wisely, in my opinion – retain the services of newly appointed NASA administrator Dan Goldin, who did all that was humanly possible to reform and revitalize NASA from the top, and who ultimately became the longest serving NASA administrator in history. Of all the things I did as head of the National Space Council, finding and recruiting Dan, and then ensuring his confirmation as Administrator in April 1992, was probably my most lasting and consequential contribution to the space program.

VIII

A LAST HURRAH?

"It's the heart afraid of breaking that never learns to dance. It is the dream afraid of waking that never takes the chance." Bette Midler

The second Bush administration, elected in 2000, was almost immediately overwhelmed by the attacks of 9/11, and its focus narrowed, appropriately so, onto the war on terror. Space exploration was a lower priority than securing the homeland and pursuing offensive actions against perpetrators of the attacks on the World Trade Center as they hid in the mountains of Afghanistan, sheltered by the Taliban regime. After nine years as NASA administrator, Dan Goldin was replaced by Sean O'Keefe, former deputy OMB director, Secretary of the Navy, Defense Comptroller, and clerk of the Senate Appropriations Committee when the Committee was under the leadership of Senator Ted Stevens of Alaska. Sean knew little of space or NASA and brought a 'comptroller's' perspective to mounting NASA costs and dwindling national returns. His tenure was primarily to be that of financial steward, caretaker and crisis avoider... until a crisis occurred.

On February 1, 2003, at 2:04pm, Eastern Standard Time, President George W. Bush addressed the United States: "This day has brought terrible news and great sadness to our country. The [space shuttle] Columbia is lost; there are no survivors." Earlier that morning, re-entering the Earth's atmosphere at the end of an otherwise routine mission, the space shuttle Columbia, and the seven crew members onboard, suddenly disintegrated. Debris from the foam-encased external fuel tank needed to lift the quarter-million pound shuttle system at launch had broken off during ascent and punched a hole in Columbia's thermal protection system, rendering the vehicle helpless to the temperatures and pressures of orbital re-entry. Despite the disaster, the President assured Americans that the space program would continue: "The cause in which they died will continue....Our journey into space will go on."[43] And Administrator O'Keefe's job transformed from "caretaker" to "care giver" for an Agency and a nation in shock from the devastating accident.

Following the loss of Columbia, the shuttle program was immediately suspended. As the space shuttles were the only delivery vehicles for space station modules, further construction on the International Space Station was also halted. Although the Station could be partially supplied using Russia's unmanned Progress vehicles, and crews were exchanged using Russian-manned Soyuz spacecraft, the Station was forced to operate with a skeleton crew of two. The human spaceflight program was clearly adrift and many questioned whether any modest gains were worth the cost and risk. After all, the Columbia was on a mission that was marginal at best. Because the shuttle Columbia was too old and too heavy to make the journey to the high inclination space station orbit, Columbia was not part of the Station assembly and resupply and was relegated to lower priority science missions and diplomatic commitments to fly foreign astronauts. The harsh fact is that the day it was lost, Columbia was meeting constituent obligations, rather than playing a central role in the primary mission of completing the Space Station.

Nevertheless, Americans' support for the space program remained strong. A national poll taken two months after the Columbia accident revealed that two-thirds believed the space shuttle should continue to fly and nearly three-quarters thought the space program was a good investment. On sending humans to Mars, 49% thought it was a good idea, while 42% opposed it. 56% supported the idea of sending civilians such as teachers into space and 38% were opposed.[44]

Less than a year after the accident, President G.W. Bush announced a new "Vision for Space Exploration," calling for the space shuttle fleet to continue flying to "fulfill our obligations to our international partners" and complete the International Space Station (ISS). The fleet would then be retired by 2010 and replaced with a newly developed Crew Exploration Vehicle for lunar orbit and landing, and then on to exploration of Mars. NASA made plans to return the space shuttle to service by September 2004, although that date was eventually pushed back to July 2005.[45]

For the second time in fifteen years, a President named Bush called on America to set a new goal for human space exploration: a return to the Moon and then on to Mars. With a Republican Congress behind him and a nation still in shock over the loss of Columbia, the time finally seemed right for a resumption of America's ambitious human space exploration program. And over the next five years solid progress on a new architecture was accomplished. But the Bush team's commitment to complete the International Space Station first and operate it for at least five years, a commitment that was part of the new vision, became a financial millstone that soon sunk the new initiative. After his election in 2008, President Obama cancelled Bush's new "Vision for Space Exploration" in favor of "leapfrog" technology development for an undefined exploration program. Obama made the decision for many reasons, relying heavily on the external work of Norman Augustine and a new committee formed to look at human spaceflight. The committee confirmed what had been true from the beginning of Bush's vision, namely that funding the status quo (shuttle and space station) *and* a bold new initiative was unaffordable. That gave President Obama an out, and top cover from a Presidential commission. Three presidencies had passed since President George H.W. Bush called for a post-Cold War exploration program to keep America advancing into the new frontier and now, for a second time, America could muster neither the will nor the wallet to answer the call.

It is an open question whether a future President will take another bite at the human space exploration apple. Frankly, it is hard to imagine. All evidence suggests that the Chinese and perhaps the Indians have taken up the gauntlet of space exploration. They are prepared to accept the costs and risks of human space exploration along with the costs of modernization, education, and infrastructure developments on the ground. Like Americans in the early 1960s, they seem committed to both and see no conflict in the resulting spending. The question for this generation of Americans is, "will we?"

———

Regardless of one's view of the ambition of the United States to reestablish its leadership and zest for human space exploration it is clear to all that changes are urgently needed at NASA for a chance of revival of the enterprise. Affecting that change, however, will be very difficult because the ranks of those that have impeded progress have grown over many years, through many administrations, and have been battle-tested time and again. And in and of themselves, changes will not guarantee a revived, focused, and successful human space exploration program, but they are necessary preconditions for success.

NASA must be entirely restructured. As part of this restructuring, NASA must first significantly limit and focus its mission. Far too many useful and interesting, but not core, civil space program missions have grown at NASA: earth science, education, information technology, even the historic aeronautics mission. These and other missions are better fits elsewhere in the federal enterprise. NASA must focus its resources exclusively on a core mission of exploration and non-Earth focused space science.

Next, NASA must dramatically reduce its center structure through the equivalent of a "base re-alignment and closure (BRAC)" process. The NASA centers, originally conceived as centers of excellence to meet very specific mission requirements, have grown into independent enterprises, diversified over time to ensure stable funding and employment. Virtually all NASA centers have ongoing activities that directly overlap the "primary missions" of other centers. This duplication and subsequent waste of effort is growing.

Third, NASA must recognize that the center of technical development and manufacturing excellence has shifted to the private sector. NASA's experience in overall program management and independent monitoring and evaluation expertise is essential and world class, but we must acknowledge as false the idea that NASA be responsible for hardware design and manufacture as part of its core missions. Recognizing this, NASA must expand its Commercial Off-The-Shelf (COTS) partnership model with a greater reliance on overall enterprise program management, insight, and technical assistance, rather than oversight and control. The Jet Propulsion Laboratory at CalTech, a "virtual

NASA center," has for decades operated successfully in this mode for robotic planetary exploration. It should serve as a model for all NASA activities in the future.

These changes will have self-reinforcing and beneficial impacts on NASA's ability to effectively and efficiently manage a human space exploration program by reducing staff and facilities, thereby reducing the need to exercise and maintain a standby NASA workforce.

Congress must support changes at NASA by encouraging and facilitating mission focus, center consolidation, and reduction. Congress must completely resist local earmarking of funds to prop up individual center activity, manning, and growth. Congress must provide permissive statutory contexts for aggressive public-private initiatives in which the government's role in development is supportive, advisory, and front-end loaded, and in which industrial partners are accountable for delivery and performance, and incentivized by reward for performance based on private investments and returns.

Artificial barriers to entry for industrial development must be reduced or eliminated. NASA must eliminate arbitrary and "protective" barriers to entry for industrial participation in expanded Commercial Off -The -Shelf (COTS) initiatives to achieve mission objectives. When the government assumes all the risk for performance under the winner take all contracting process, a "fly before you buy," test and test again and barriers to entry for past performance make sense. However, when pay is based on performance, performance risk shifts to contractors and the government simply ensures overall enterprise risk management through insight, backup, and diversification.

The test for participation should be limited to an ability to finance a significant portion of development and operations cost and reasonable demonstration of capability and capacity; the test should not primarily be demonstrations of "past performance". This will encourage the formation of new industrial teams and will force legacy NASA contractors to adapt or atrophy (a process that is already getting underway, although slowly).

Private industry should be incentivized to bring world class capabilities to exploration, including international partnerships based purely on financing and technical capability rather than on "foreign policy" considerations. International participation should be based primarily on private sector efficiencies rather than on government-to-government arrangements. Thresholds that put emphasis on US-led enterprises are warranted, given the objectives of developing and sustaining an industrial base and the significant investment of the US government. However, US-led industrial teams should not be restricted in utilizing "best of breed" technologies and facilities comprised of foreign industrial partners.

NASA is one of America's most prized institutions. It has been at the center of our proudest achievements as a world-leading nation. It has piloted a technology revolution that fueled the greatest economic expansion in human history. And it has been a beacon for generations of aspiring American youth. As an institution, it can rise to those heights again, but to do so will require a sober self-assessment, a desire to change, and a willingness to let go of what has long brought institutional comfort at the expense of national achievement.

EPILOGUE

In July 1991 I hosted a dinner for the leaders of America's space community. Scientists, industrialists, government executives, journalists, and authors were all in attendance. The dinner was part of the White House's effort to help energize interest and enthusiasm for President Bush's new Space Exploration Initiative, and to make sure that all knew the President was serious about the initiative and why. At one point in the evening, Carl Sagan was sitting on a couch in our living room with our youngest daughter, Olivia, then almost nine years old. Carl was a remarkable man, gentle and thoughtful, a born teacher and good friend. He and Olivia were engaged in deep conversation for a while and later, I asked her what she was talking to Carl about.

"I asked him why he was so interested in exploring space," she answered. "He said, 'I believe that the answer to the question, "Is there life anywhere except on Earth in the whole Universe?" will be the single most significant, and profound piece of information ever to be discovered in the history of man. And it doesn't matter whether the answer is "Yes" or "No" – either way, it will be the most important discovery in human history. I want to be a part of the search for that answer, and I want to be right at the front of the line when we open that door."

Over the years, and especially while at the Space Council, I have spent a great deal of time and thought on finding the most compelling case to be made for human space exploration. I have been through every "Tang and Teflon" argument, I have looked at thousands of children's drawings of astronauts and space ships and examined graph after graph of engineering enrollments. I have seen the economic forecasts for mining helium 3 on the Moon and for beaming solar power to Earth using acre-sized solar collectors in low Earth orbit and powerful lasers to beam the energy to surface collectors. Simply put, as a rationale to spend billions of earthly dollars on an expedition through the Solar System and beyond, Carl's line of reasoning is the best. It is simple, clear, and compelling. After all, great nations should address great questions and the greatest nations should address the greatest question. But my observation is this is not primarily what moves nations to explore. Rather, it is power, wealth, and prestige that move nations to explore, and as long as there is power, wealth, and prestige to be had, nations will explore. There was a time when the United States instinctively pursued the aim of human space exploration, and in my mind the dividends it earned on all three scores were priceless. Today the Chinese and the Indians are retracing steps we took decades ago, in pursuit of the same goals: power, wealth, and prestige. They are spending vast sums and taking incalculable risks simply to follow in our footsteps in hopes of retracing them – and then going beyond. This mystifies those of us who take the "been there, done that" attitude. But for others, the aims of these countries are clear and unmistakable. After all, who wants to be the marquee name in the twenty-first century as America was in the twentieth? I think and hope that we still do.

Perhaps the titanic philosophical, economic, and military conflict of the Cold War inflated the drama and importance of the great space race so much so that we never could sustain it without the greater story line. There was so much riding on every step on the path to space that we were willing to invest almost anything to keep in front: our time, our talent, our treasure, and our collective ego. And the enterprise itself never failed to rise to mythic storytelling height. It had it all: triumph, failure, suspense, love, and even hate for the dreaded Soviet Union. Footprints on the moon, tragedy on the launch pad, an embrace and handshake in the heavens, the narcissistic first glimpse of our own reflection in the celestial mirror. Maybe it was too much to sustain after the great competition of the twentieth century drew to a peaceful close.

In my book, everyone who played a part in the final chapter of the great space race and the end of the Cold War were heroes. There were no "good guys" and no "bad guys," only people trying to do the best for the enterprise from the vantage point of the role in which they were cast. I have no regrets and I suspect none of the others involved do either.

Along the way I was blessed to know some incredible human beings who made enormous contributions to history, and they are far too numerous to mention them all. From President George H. W. Bush and his Vice President, Dan Quayle, and the entire White House team who shared and encouraged a vision for a new space enterprise even while they were peacefully navigating an entire world in the process of fundamentally transforming; to Carl Sagan and Edward Teller, old and committed adversaries who remarkably made common cause in the advancement of a vision for space after the Cold War. From Roald Sagdeev, Anatoly Kiselev, and Yuri Koptiev, who brought the Russian space program through the end of the Soviet regime to a new future, to leaders of American industry like Norm Augustine, Bill Anders, John McDonnell, and Stan Pace, who helped transform and preserve American technological strength through the largest military stand-down in history. From the Apollo and Mercury astronauts, my childhood heroes, to Gene Roddenberry and Ray Bradbury, who took NASA's actual small steps and embroidered them into American mythologies and legends for our age. From legendary and colorful members of Congress, like John Tower, Jake Garn, Barbara Mikulski, Al Gore, and, of course, my boss and mentor Pete Wilson, to the extraordinary men and women of NASA and the NASA centers, upon whose shoulders many of the great technical victories of the Cold War rest. And finally, from people like Tom Paine, Dick Truly, J.R. Thompson, Dan Goldin, Sean O'Keefe and Mike Griffin, household names who led the civil space program through this period, to Ben Shriever, Jim Abrahamson, Don Kutyna, Tom Morman and Jimmy Hill, unknown to most Americans who quietly and without fanfare pushed the envelope of freedom in space from behind the veils of secrecy.

America has tried twice now, since the end of the Cold War, to toss our collective caps over the next wall. In 1989 we were unable to make a commitment that stuck, and I am fearful that we will not make it this time either. I will leave it to the psycho-sociologists to interpret what means for America and where we are in our national life cycle, but I know that humans won't stop exploring space and will continue to expand our footprint in space. The United States may well lead that venture, or participate in it, or, most sadly of all, simply watch it. It's up to all of us.

(ENDNOTES)

1. Quayle Says Buchanan Is Out of Step; Vice President Takes Up Gauntlet on Right; *E. J. Dionne Jr.*. The Washington Post Washington, D.C.: Dec 19, 1991. pg. a.18

2. "Nomination of John G.Tower to be Secretary of Defense, Hearings before the Committee on Armed Services United States Senate, One Hundred and First Congress, First Session." February 23, 1989. 341-79.

3. On April 20, 1989, President Bush signed Executive Order 12675 establishing "The National Space Council";

Section I. Establishment and Composition of the National Space Council.

(a) There is established the National Space Council ("the Council").

(b) The Council shall be composed of the following members:

(1) The Vice President, who shall be Chairman of the Council;

(2) The Secretary of State;

(3) The Secretary of the Treasury;

(4) The Secretary of Defense;

(5) The Secretary of Commerce;

(6) The Secretary of Transportation;

(7) The Director of the Office of Management and Budget;

(8) The Chief of Staff to the President;

(9) The Assistant to the President for National Security Affairs;

(10) The Assistant to the President for Science and Technology;

(11) The Director of Central Intelligence; and

(12) The Administrator of the National Aeronautics and Space Administration.

(c) The Chairman shall, from time to time, invite the following to participate in meetings of the Council:

(1) The Chairman of the Joint Chiefs of Staff; and

(2) The heads of other executive departments and agencies and other senior officials in the Executive Office of the President.

Sec. 2. Functions of the Council. (a) The Council shall advise and assist the President on national space policy and strategy, and perform such other duties as the President may from time to time prescribe.

(b) In addition, the Council is directed to:

(1) review United States Government space policy, including long-range goals, and develop a strategy for national space activities;

(2) develop recommendations for the President on space policy and space- related issues;

(3) monitor and coordinate implementation of the objectives of the President's national space policy by executive departments and agencies; and

(4) foster close coordination, cooperation, and technology and information exchange among the civil, national security, and commercial space sectors, and facilitate resolution of differences concerning major space and space-related policy issues.

(c) The creation and operation of the Council shall not interfere with existing lines of authority and responsibilities in the departments and agencies.

Sec. 3. Responsibilities of the Chairman. (a) The Chairman shall serve as the President's principal advisor on national space policy and strategy.

(b) The Chairman shall, in consultation with the members of the Council, establish procedures for the Council and establish the agenda for Council activities.

(c) The Chairman shall report to the President on the activities and recommendations of the Council. The Chairman shall advise the Council as appropriate regarding the President's directions with respect to the Council's activities and national space policy generally.

(d) The Chairman shall authorize the establishment of such committees of the Co uncil, including an executive committee, and of such working groups, composed o f senior designees of the Council members and of other officials invited to par ticipate in Council meetings, as he deems necessary or appropriate for the effi cient conduct of Council functions.

Sec. 4. National Space Policy Planning Process. (a) The Council will establish a process for developing and monitoring the implementation of national space policy and strategy.

(b) To implement this process, each agency represented on the Council shall provide such information regarding its current and planned space activities as the Chairman shall request.

(c) The head of each executive department and agency shall ensure that its space-related activities conform to national space policy and strategy.

Sec. 5. Establishment of Vice President's Space Policy Advisory Board. (a) The Vice President shall establish, in accordance with the provisions of the Federal Advisory Committee Act, as amended (5 U.S.C. App. 2), governing Presidential advisory committees, an advisory committee of private citizens to advise the Vice President on the space policy of the United States ("the Board").

(b) The Board shall be composed and function as follows:

(1) The Board shall be composed of members appointed by the Vice President.

(2) The Vice President shall designate a Chairman from among the members of the Board. The Executive Secretary of the National Space Council shall serve as the Secretary to the Board.

(3) Members of the Board shall serve without any compensation for their work on the Board. However, they shall be entitled to travel expenses, including per diem in lieu of subsistence, as authorized by law, for persons serving intermittently in the Government service (5 U.S.C. 5701-5707), to the extent funds are available for that purpose.

(4) Necessary expenses of the Board shall be paid from funds available for the expenses of the National Space Council.

(5) Notwithstanding the provisions of any other Executive order, the responsibilities of the President under the Federal Advisory Committee Act, as amended, except that of reporting annually to the Congress, which are applicable to the Board established by this order, shall be performed on a reimbursable basis by the Director of the Office of Administration in the Executive Office of the President, in accordance with the guidelines and procedures established by the Administrator of General Services.

Sec. 6. Microgravity Research Board. Section 1(c) of Executive Order No. 12660 is amended by deleting "Economic Policy Council" and inserting in lieu thereof "National Space Council." Sec. 7. Administrative Provisions. (a) The Office of Administration in the Executive Office of the President shall provide the Council with such administrative support on a reimbursable basis as may be necessary for the performance of the functions of the Council.

(b) The President shall appoint an Executive Secretary who shall appoint such staff as may be necessary to assist in the performance of the Council's functions.

(c) All Federal departments, agencies, and interagency councils and committees having an impact on space policy shall extend, as appropriate, such cooperation and assistance to the Council as is necessary to carry out its responsibilities under this order.

(d) The head of each agency serving on the Council or represented on any working group or committee of the Council shall provide such administrative support as may be necessary, in accordance with law and subject to the availability of appropriations, to enable the agency head or its representative to carry out his responsibilities.

Sec. 8. Report. The Council shall submit an annual report setting forth its assessment of and recommendations for the space policy and strategy of the United States Government.

4. Paul Hoversten. "Council Chief is Known as Top Defense Expert." *Florida Today*. March 3, 1989.

5. Bruce Reed. "Rocket Man." *The New Republic*. May16, 1989.

6. Elliot Marshall. "An Arbitrator for Space Policy." *The Economist*. March 10, 1989.

7. "Albrecht Named to National Space Council; Military Background Concerns Some." *Satellite Week*. March 6, 1989.

8. National Academy of Science. "Toward a New Era In Space: A Report to President-Elect George Bush." December, 1988.

9. George Bush and Brent Scowcroft. *A World Transformed*. New York: Knopf, 1998. 43.

10. Bush and Scowcroft, 73.

11. Thor Hogan. *Mars Wars: The Rise and Fall of the Space Exploration Initiative*. NASA: 2007. 66.

12. Washington Post, July 12, 1989, Evans and Novak, "Quayle's Ambitious Space Program."

13. Aeronautics and Space Engineering Board (ASEB). "Human Exploration of Space: A Review of NASA's 90-Day Study and Alternatives." ASEB: 1990. 7.

14. Kathy Sawyer. "Quayle to Give NASA Competition On Ideas for Space Exploration." *The Washington Post*. November 17, 1989. A21

15. *New York Times*. November 10, 1989.

16. *Wall Street Journal*. November 10, 1989. Opinion Page.

17. Bush and Scowcroft, pg. 149

18. Bush and Scowcroft, 150.

19. "Gorbachev's Speech at the Congress." Russian Information Agency (ITAR-TASS). May 30, 1989.

20. Bush and Scowcroft, 154.

21. Bush and Scowcroft, 169.

22.   Bush and Scowcroft, 150.

23.   Roald Sagdeev. The Making of a Soviet Scientist. New York: John Wiley & Sons, 1994.

24.   Sagdeev, 267.

25.   Sagdeev, 267.

26.   Sagdeev, 266.

27.   Sagdeev, 269.

28.   Susan Eisenhower. *Partners in Space: US-Russian Cooperation After the Cold War.* The Eisenhower Institute, 2004. 18-20.

29.   "Agreement Between the United States of America and the Union of Soviet Socialist Republics Concerning Cooperation in the Exploration and Use of Outer Space for Peaceful Purposes." Signed in April 1987. The agreement is implemented by the U.S. National Aeronautics and Space Administration (NASA) and the U.S.S.R. Academy of Science.

30.   Almost five years later, when NASA faced imminent cancellation of the bloated Space Station, new NASA administrator Dan Goldin – who had earned the trust and respect of the Clinton administration by demonstrating his loyalty and ability to work within White House guidance – was given the authority to utilize Russian capabilities to the fullest extent in order to radically change the Space Station design and function, carving millions of dollars from the budget and years off the delivery schedule.

31.   John Dowdy. "Winners and Losers in the Arms Industry Downturn." *Foreign Policy* 107 (Summer, 1997). 88.

32.   Bush and Scowcroft, 276.

33.   "Cheney Gives Plan to Reduce Forces by 25% in 5 years." *Washington Post.* June 19, 1990.

34.   Bush and Scowcroft, 302-3.

35.   Bush and Scowcroft, 318.

36.   The account of Lockheed's entrance into the Khrunichev partnership was provided by Mel Brashears and is used with his permission.

37.   Accounts of this trip were provided by Mel Brashears and is used with his permission.

38.   The entire account of this meeting is provided by Valery Pivarov, who attended the meeting and provided translation services; although edited for smooth reading, this is entirely his work and is used with his permission.

39.   Susan Eisenhower, in her book *Partners in Space*, speculates that Kiselev's hiring of
       Yeltsin's daughter, Tatiana was instrumental in gaining concessions for the forma-
       tion of Khrunichev (40).

40.   The breakup of Soviet industries into privatized entities in the early 1990s was a
       messy process led by Yeltsin and managed by his principal deputy, Anatoly Chubias.
       Chubias was a brilliant young technocrat whose rapid dismantling of Soviet-era
       industries was derisively termed by many as the new "Russian kleptocracy." Yeltsin
       and Chubias have been roundly criticized for the manner and speed of the privatiza-
       tion that most have associated with the rise of the oligarchs and organized crime in
       the new Russia. In 1998 I attended a private dinner with Chubias where he was asked
       specifically about his regrets regarding the rapid and somewhat haphazard privatiza-
       tion process. Chubias expressed no regrets and explained that Yeltsin and his team
       faced a difficult choice in 1991. With a volatile situation in Russia, they faced two
       stark alternatives. One was a measured and studied approach to privatizing Soviet-
       era industries and infrastructure with more consistent industrial themes, real com-
       petition, and competent management which would take time and political capital
       to analyze, adjudicate, and implement. Or, they could divest quickly and somewhat
       haphazardly, recognizing that the opportunities for corruption and malfeasance
       would be large. For Yeltsin and Chubias, the choice was easy. In their view the high-
       est priority for Russia was to reject Soviet Communism rapidly and completely, with-
       out a possibility of reversion. And as the merciless murder of the Romanovs by the
       Bolsheviks instantly and irrevocably slammed the door on a return of the aristocracy,
       the new Russia would effectively dismantle Soviet Communism in one fell swoop. It
       was messy and ruthless, and completely effective. Yeltsin and Chubias knew exactly
       what they were doing and never regretted it.

41.   The Arms Export Control Act (AECA) was amended in 1996 to cover brokering
       activity by all persons (except officers/employees of the USG acting in an official
       capacity) with respect to the manufacture, export, import, or transfer of any defense
       articles or defense service on the U.S. Munitions List of the ITAR. Activities before
       1996 were not covered by this law.

42.   These meetings were typically short and to the point, although, as we came to
       discover, the Russians have a tendency to believe that volume and detail in and of
       themselves can provide a compelling rationale for their point of view and position.
       I witnessed this firsthand years earlier when Senator Wilson and I were informal
       observers of the Defense and Space Talks between the United States and the Soviet

Union in Geneva in the late 1980s. Our delegation would frequently complain of their Soviet counterparts' long and detailed presentations on one particular point or another. Even social functions we attended would frequently include long and tedious expostulations on one particular issue or another.

43. President George Bush. "The Space Shuttle Columbia Tragedy." Speech to the nation delivered February 1, 2003, from the White House Cabinet Room.

44. Angus Reid Public Opinion. "Humans in Space Important for Americans." July 30, 2003. <http://www.angus-reid.com/polls/27077/humans_in_space_important_for_americans/>

45. Presidential speech at NASA Headquarters, Washington, D.C. on January 14, 2004.

INDEX